# Recipe
*for a*
# Blue Ribbon School

# Recipe
## *for a*
# Blue Ribbon School

A STEP-BY-STEP GUIDE TO CREATING A POSITIVE SCHOOL
CLIMATE WHILE IMPROVING STUDENT ACHIEVEMENT

## Brent Walker,

MS in Education with 30 years experience in education

iUniverse, Inc.
New York Lincoln Shanghai

**Recipe for a Blue Ribbon School**
A STEP-BY-STEP GUIDE TO CREATING A POSITIVE SCHOOL
CLIMATE WHILE IMPROVING STUDENT ACHIEVEMENT

iUniverse books may be ordered through booksellers or by contacting:

iUniverse
2021 Pine Lake Road, Suite 100
Lincoln, NE 68512
www.iuniverse.com
1-800-Authors (1-800-288-4677)

The views expressed in this work are solely those of the author and
do not necessarily reflect the views of the publisher, and the publisher hereby
disclaims any responsibility for them.

ISBN-13: 978-0-595-40956-3 (pbk)
ISBN-13: 978-0-595-85315-1 (ebk)
ISBN-10: 0-595-40956-3 (pbk)
ISBN-10: 0-595-85315-3 (ebk)

Printed in the United States of America

*This book could not have been written without the unending support, help, and encouragement of my wife, Nancy, and my son, Brent Michael. I dedicate this work to them, with all my love.*

# CONTENTS

# INTRODUCTION

I have been the principal of Westside Elementary in Powell, Wyoming, for the past 23 years. In 1999, the Wyoming Department of Education started testing all fourth-grade students in the state using the WyCAS achievement test for math, reading, and writing. In 1999, out of the 207 Wyoming elementary schools, Westside students scored in the average range for the state. In 2003, our students scored first in math, sixth in reading, and seventh in writing. In 2004, the United States Department of Education recognized Westside as a No Child Left Behind Blue Ribbon School for High Achievement. We were one of 256 public and private, elementary, middle and high schools across the nation to receive this honor. Westside's recognition has led me to help other schools with school improvement. As I provide staff development and present at national conferences, I am often asked if I have written material to share. This book is the result of those requests.

In the past couple of years, staff members from over eighteen different schools have visited Westside. Similar comments have come from every visiting group. A visiting school board member said, "I can't believe how much your students want to learn," and a visiting fifth-grade teacher said, "I just can't believe how well-behaved your students are." What people see when they visit Westside is the culmination of several years of work and change. What they leave with is a picture of how their school can look.

Westside became a Blue Ribbon School because we really started to believe that all kids can learn. We made a paradigm shift in how we taught as a result of following two guiding principles: first, instruction will be driven by the use of data, and second, different amounts of learning time will be provided for every student. What is unique about Westside is how we actually put the philosophy that all kids can learn into action using these two principles.

This book spells out how we took research and applied it to become a Blue Ribbon School. Each chapter details a different change that took place so our actions could align with our philosophy. You will not find a chapter on staff development or instructional approaches. It is assumed that you are already following and using current research in both of these areas.

The changes outlined here did not occur overnight. When I work with other schools, I start out by saying that this is a three-year to five-year process because you are changing how you think and how you view education. In other words, many of the changes require a paradigm shift in how the staff thinks and how the staff uses time. While this may sound imposing, it is not an impossible task. It is one that is well worth the time and effort. The benefits to students, staff, and parents go far beyond better test scores.

Visiting staff have also made the following comments: "I can't believe how well your staff works together," and "The atmosphere is so positive, for everyone." These comments illustrate the collaboration that now takes place between the staff members and that the learning environment, the school climate, has changed for all of us.

Each chapter addresses a component that has contributed to Westside's success. I recommend reading the whole book first and then rereading the chapters that most intimately relate to your school's needs. The kind of change that visiting staff members want for their school will not come from a single change; it is a process that involves all facets of the school. You cannot work on just one area without impacting the others.

I refer to some specific programs and books in order to illuminate how their ideas are being used. It is how they are being used that is important, not what they are. For most schools, buying a new textbook, new test materials, a new computer program, or a new "boxed" program will not lead to the type of change required by No Child Left Behind. Real change requires you to start using what you already have differently. There is a saying that I like to use, "If you keep doing what you have always done, you will continue to get what you have always gotten." True change requires trust, courage, and stamina. It is my hope that this book will help you decide to take the road to true change.

# 1

# WHY SCHOOLS NEED TO CHANGE

The need for educational change is greater now than ever before. Education has always been the necessary vehicle for improving a person's ability to change social groups or to better oneself. As the United States developed as a nation, the education system changed to meet the new needs for an educated workforce.

## How Education Developed

Dr. Lezotte, in his book, *The Effective Schools Process*, points out that, as the United States was forming, we had a predominantly agricultural society. At that time, ninety percent of the people lived off the land. Families were large in order to provide additional workers for the farm. During this time, the United States became the greatest agricultural producer in the world. Paralleling this age was the premise that education was for some people but, definitely, not for all. Reading, writing and math were for an elite group. Education was primarily classical: literature, Latin, math, and geography. This system worked well until the 1800's and the onset of the industrial age.

In the industrial age, many of the migrants from the agricultural age moved directly into the factory. All they needed was a strong back and a good work ethic and not a lot of education. The industrial age also required a new group of people, middle management. This new group of workers needed more education. To provide a more educated workforce, compulsory education for all and learning for some was born.

The driving force in compulsory education was attendance. In most cases, what students knew when they finished twelve years of schooling was never measured, yet their attendance was measured daily, even hourly. The basic course of study also changed. The classical education gave way, with much turmoil, to vocational education. Science replaced Latin. Reading became a skill-based curriculum in place of a study of literature. The curriculum continued to change as the need for more workers that were highly educated increased. As the world continued to decrease in size, becoming a global economy, and the United States factories started to compete with other nations for goods produced in the factory, the industrial age was left behind and the communication age was born.

## We Enter the Communication Age

The communication age requires a totally different kind of skilled worker. The skills of the industrial age—a strong back, good work ethic and some education—do not transfer to the communication age. To meet the work force needs of this new age, education has changed. Education no longer requires compulsory attendance for all and learning for some; it is now compulsory learning for all.

As we become part of a global economy, the industrial factories have been forced to move overseas. The economics of running a factory, the cost of labor, insurance, and raw materials, have made it impossible to continue producing many goods in the United States. The need for a more educated work force has risen. This new work force requires that everyone be well educated. The jobs that are expanding and pay the higher salaries are the ones that require higher-level thinking skills and stronger communication skills.

Education for all is no longer just knowing a lot of facts. The abilities to think, use information from many sources, make an informed decision, and communicate that decision to others are paramount. Being able to read for information, to use math at a higher level, and to write intelligently as a communication tool are the skills needed by today's workforce. Schools are just now starting to transition from compulsory attendance to compulsory learning.

No Child Left Behind is perhaps the most visible example of this change. The controversy seems to come primarily, not from suggesting that all students learn (no group is willing to say that some students cannot learn), but from the fact that educators have to change their basic expectations. Educators, for the first time in history, are now accountable for all students learning, instead of just attendance. This means that they have to change from teaching students and taking attendance to ensuring that all students actually learn. Most school policy books were full of policies aimed at keeping students in school, but those same policy books were void of any mention of what students were required to know when they left school. Graduation credit was awarded as a Carnegie Unit based on the amount of time spent in each class. The assumption was that time spent in the classroom was equal to what a student learned.

## Teaching for a Global Economy

In the compulsory attendance age, teachers could choose what they taught, with little regard to what students learned. When one looks at the number of students who graduated after twelve years of education who could not do basic math or read above a third-grade level, it is hard to say the students received an educa-tion. In the industrial age, this was acceptable because that group could usually find a good job, leading to a middle-class income, in the factories, the oil fields, auto industry, etc. Thomas L. Friedman, in his book "*The World is Flat*," examines how ten forces are flatten-ing the world, explaining how the world is becoming a true global economy. It is these forces that are requiring schools to change what they are teaching.

> Jobs that can be digitized are moving overseas.

We now have a global economy. Many of the middle-class jobs of the industrial age have either moved overseas or are in the process of moving overseas because it is less expensive to produce the same product elsewhere. The steel, clothing, and oil industries, to name a few, have fled the United States. We complain about the loss of jobs in the United States, then go to WalMart and stock-up on all the inexpensive items imported from China, Taiwan, Korea, and other areas where costs are low. As a nation, we are not willing to pay more for goods just to retain jobs.

The middle-class jobs that most people held in the industrial age are either gone or disappearing due to our global economy and the onset of the communication age. If a person's job or parts of a person's job can be digitized, it will be outsourced to a nation like India which has a highly educated work force, very low wages, and access to the rest of the world through the computer.

The global economy has changed the goals of the educational system. Middle-class jobs that required a good work ethic, a strong back, and some education have moved overseas and will not be returning. Our education system must change to meet the new requirements brought about by the communication age. The abilities to access information, use information from many sources, and be able to communicate with others are the new skills on which schools need to focus. Schools must give all students the basic skills plus teach them how to think and to communicate. The middle-class jobs of tomorrow, which may not even exist today, will require a more highly-educated population.

# No Child Left Behind

In the 2003 No Child Left Behind law, the federal government extended the reach of the old Title I laws and added teeth to the Title I act of 1995. No Child Left Behind came about because the states refused to take the Title I act of 1995 seriously. The Title I act required all states to develop high standards for reading and math for all Title I schools. The standards were to be a list of things a student could be expected to do in reading and math at the end of fourth, eighth, and eleventh grades. When states failed to develop those standards, No Child Left Behind was born.

No Child Left Behind requires all states to develop those standards and to assess how well all students in grades four, eight, and eleven in the state are meeting those standards. In 2006, No Child Left Behind was expanded to grades three through eight and eleven. By 2014, all third through eighth and eleventh-grade students in every state will be required to be proficient on their state test in reading and math. Each year, every school and district has to make average yearly progress toward meeting the 2014 goal. Failure to meet average yearly progress results in a number of sanctions, over a period of time, from the school providing a tutor to the removal of the total staff. The goal of the federal government was, on one level, to get states to change their educational system from the industrial age to the communication age.

Many states and their district officers, in an effort to help schools meet average yearly progress, are setting their "Cut" scores, the score a student must achieve to be proficient on the assessment, at a low level so that the majority of schools will meet average yearly progress without making a lot of changes. This stance allows schools and teachers to continue to teach the same as they always have without getting into average yearly progress jeopardy. The fallacy with this line of action is readily apparent when one compares the state test scores with scores from the NAEP test, National Assessment of Educational Progress. NAEP is required by the United States Department of Education to be given to a sample of all fourth-grade, eighth-grade, and twelfth-grade students in every state. The results are reported in the same manner as all the required state tests; the percent of students scoring novice, basic, proficient, or advanced. When one compares the results of the NAEP against the state test results, you can see which states have made a state test that is much easier than the NAEP. Right now, states are allowed to use their state test when computing average yearly progress. I wonder how long the federal government will allow this, when the same students score 80% proficient on the state test and only 20% proficient on the NAEP.

# All Students Can Learn

In the communication age, we must ensure that all students learn. To accomplish this goal, we can use three facts about learning that we have always known: first, students come to school with different backgrounds; second, students learn at different rates; and third, learning is incremental. In the industrial age, these facts did not really matter. For the most part, students entered school in first grade, behaved and attended, and left after twelve years. To ensure that all students actually learn, schools and educators must now pay close attention to these three facts and address them in their teaching and school structure.

Schools have been slow to adapt to the new requirements for education, preparing students for the communication age. Many educators do not see or understand the need for change. School systems are designed and educators have been trained to prepare students for the industrial age. To truly ensure that all students learn requires the entire educational system to change, including the district, each school and all staff.

# 2

# MAKING TIME A VARIABLE

Westside had been a high-achieving school for many years prior to Wyoming requiring all fourth-grade, eighth-grade, and eleventh-grade students to take the state achievement test. As a high-achieving school, all of our classes were consistently averaging at or above the 70th percentile on the norm-referenced Terra Nova test given at the end of each year. We thought that we were really doing a great job. In retrospect, we were just coasting along. We were teaching those students in the upper and upper-middle groups and even pushing a few students from the low-middle group into the third and fourth quartile on the Terra Nova test. We had even changed a number of programs, textbooks and teaching styles, but the overall results and class averages on the Terra Nova remained the same. The only real change was which group of students scored high or low. For example, when we went to the whole language concept, the students who had been scoring low on reading, our global learners, started scoring in the top two quartiles, while the analytic learners who required phonics, dropped into the second quartile.

The state of Wyoming required all schools to start developing and teaching to standards in the 90's. In 1999, when the first state-wide test of fourth graders was given, Westside scored just above the middle when compared to the other 209 elementary schools in Wyoming. When the staff and I looked at those first results, we concluded that they were not good enough and that we needed to improve. Our previous experience with changing textbooks, programs, and instruction helped us understand that we could not make the kind of change needed to reach 100% proficient by just doing more of the same. Looking at the Effective Schools research on increasing the amount of academic engaged time, we started to think about changing the amount of academic time students received.

# Changing Structure to Increase Learning Time

Westside had already made a number of structural changes to get more academic time. About 60% of our students ride a bus to school. When the district added fifteen minutes to our day so the high school could meet the minimum minutes required by the state, we decided to use those minutes in a different manner. When students get to school, they line up by class outside their classroom door. When the bell rings, the teacher joins the students, and they all walk the quarter mile around the school playground. Using the new fifteen minutes this way actually gave us much more academically engaged time.

During the morning walk, the students and teacher are encouraged to visit with one another. The teacher sets a lively pace, so students get their heart rate up and all the kinks from the morning bus ride are worked out. When the teacher and students enter school after the walk, coats are quickly hung-up, seats are taken and academic time is in full swing because the students are ready to learn. For a few students, these fifteen minutes became extra reading time. By giving reading instruction during the walk time, these students do not miss any classroom academic time.

We also looked at our lunch program. We decided that too much time was being spent in the classroom "discussing" what had happened during the noon recess. We shortened recess by five minutes and moved recess before lunch. Students now go to recess for fifteen minutes, come in and wash their hands, then go to lunch. This switch yielded three benefits: first, our waste from lunch went from three big containers to just over one–the students had started to eat their lunch. The second benefit was increased learning time. All the discussions generated during recess are talked out during lunch. When students return to the classroom after lunch, it is academic time. We have given them time to visit about all the exploits at recess. Now, it is our time for learning. The third benefit was creating a positive culture in which lunch is now a social time for the students. It is a bit noisier, but the noise is appropriate. If my wife and I go to dinner with friends, we all visit during dinner. When the students go to lunch, it is very similar. They are engaged in social conversation.

# Eliminating Some Recess Increases Academic Time

For some time, the fourth-grade and fifth-grade teachers had been concerned about not having a long block of uninterrupted class time. To give them up to a two-hour block of time, I permanently removed the fifteen-minute afternoon recess for fourth and fifth graders. This block of time, without any interruptions, allows the teachers to work on application problems and cross-curricular projects requiring a large amount of time. It also gives the teachers an extra seventy-five minutes a week. First through third grades kept their mid-morning and mid-afternoon recess because of their developmental levels.

Unfortunately, while these changes did provide us with more academic time, that time did not translate into substantially higher achievement. It did change our school climate in a positive manner. Students were begin-ning to be more respectful of our learn-ing time. Some stu-dents were starting to take learning a bit more seriously. The staff was being more careful about how they used time. However, we still needed to get more time for those students who were not being successful.

> Changing the school structure, how the day is scheduled, became a paradigm shift.

The results from the initial fourth-grade state test, WyCAS, generated several long discussions. We decided that, while we could not change the length of the day, we could change how we used the time we already had. This was an easy con-cept, but one that required major changes in how we operated. The first step was to start using the data we already had on what students knew and what they did not know. Using that data, we developed our at-risk plan, which gave identified students more time to learn. Westside had the same amount of time that everyone else had, but how we used it became very different.

## Accelerated Reading Facilitates Change

Changing time isn't just a matter of adding an after-school tutor or an early-morn-ing work session. It isn't just eliminating a recess or shortening lunch. It is chang-ing how you think about what is important and what isn't. It is about changing schedules, programs, and instructional methods to meet individual student needs. Chapter 3, *At-Risk*, covers many changes that can be easily accomplished by mak-ing changes in the schedule. Chapter 4, *Using Data to Focus Instruction*, explains how data guides those changes.

To actually change how time is used takes much more than changing the schedule. It actually requires a change in how teachers think and act. An example of using time differently and changing how teachers think and behave is dem-onstrated by our use of the Accelerated Reading program. In many ways, the Accelerated Reading program has helped the Westside staff grow into using time differently.

When I first brought the Accelerated Reading program into Westside, I had to convince the two third-grade teachers to use it. At first, it was on one machine in the library. I purposely put the testing machine in the library because I wanted the students to leave the classroom and come to the library to do their testing. I wanted to break the cycle of "the teacher controls everything." Slowly, the third-grade teachers let go of their control and allowed students the freedom to go to the library, unattended, to take the computerized tests. As the students started doing better, in reading and in behavior, other grade-level teachers started their students on the Accelerated Reading program.

I started to really push the program as we got more data showing how much better the students were doing in reading. As the program grew, I put more computers in the library so students did not have to wait to take tests. Soon, all the grades, except kindergarten, allowed students to go to the library to take tests and to check out books as the students had time during the day. The students now had control over part of their learning. This was a change in the structure of Westside. The library was now being used all of the time, not just thirty minutes a week under the control of the schedule. The teachers were beginning to trust their students to do the right thing. The students rewarded the teachers by doing the right thing.

Most of the reading for the Accelerated Reading program was being done at home. This helped extend the school day without adding more work to the teacher's load. The Accelerated Reading program also had the effect of differentiating reading. Students read books at their appropriate reading level, using home time to practice the skill of reading.

Now that the third grade teachers had confidence in the Accelerated Reading program, I convinced them to pilot the Reading Renaissance program. The Reading Renaissance program means that the students do silent, independent reading for thirty to forty-five minutes a day in the classroom while the teacher closely monitors and adjusts the level of books being read. The first year, the third-grade teachers gave me one semester based on trust. The next year, they used Reading Renaissance the whole year based on the data from the previous year. The following year, the whole school implemented the Reading Renaissance program.

At this point, several goals were accomplished: the library was being used daily by all the grades; teachers were trusting their students to go to the library to take tests and check out books without being closely supervised; students were taking responsibility for their actions; technology was being used to provide teachers with accurate data on how well the students were reading; teachers were learning how to use and trust up-to-the-minute data; we were extending the learning time because students were required to do their reading homework every night at home; and finally, everyone was having fun because we were all being successful. The students were finding success with their reading and earning points to use during shopping day, and the teachers were being successful because the students were doing much better with their reading.

As the program grew, the need for more computer stations grew. Several teachers began complaining about the long wait in the library before a student could take an Accelerated Reading test, sometimes a couple of days. This led to the development of a simple network which allowed centralized data collection for the Accelerated Reading program. The library computers and additional computers were moved into the classrooms. All this happened over a period of five years.

## Teachers' Attitudes Toward Learning Changed

Again, looking back, the most important thing that happened was the change in teachers' attitudes toward teaching and learning. The teachers found that time could be used differently, students could learn without the teachers teaching in the front of the room, and the use of data helps accelerate learning.

The idea that time can be a variable has changed the culture at Westside. We evaluate all activities and changes based on time. The question asked is, "Are we or will we be wasting a student's time?" Wasting time is defined as: "Are we teaching the student something the student already knows?" If the answer is yes, we either stop doing it or never begin doing it.

As we have gotten better at asking and answering that question, we have found that change becomes more of the norm. When we look at a student's assessment results and focus on teaching what the student does not know, lessons change. The Accelerated Reading and Reading Renaissance programs helped increase student comprehension, but we still needed to provide more time to re-teach basic skills in reading and math.

## Flexible Action Grouping Helps All Students

The real change in time came with the development of our flexible action grouping, which is fully described in Chapter 5. Flexible action grouping has helped students achieve mastery sooner and to retain the skills being taught. This has led to more instructional time, which has led to teaching more application of skills already mastered, which has led to better retention of skills, which—well, you get the point. Because of the many ways we are now using time differently, we are able to make changes in sched-

> **Flexible grouping gives instructional time to all students.**

ules and instruction very quickly to respond to student needs based on our data. Even at the first grade, we are not covering more standards, but we are able to teach students more application of those standards. As students begin entering the next grade at or above grade level in reading and math, the teacher actually gains time each year because there is not a need to spend time reviewing and re-teaching before starting on new material.

An academic example comes from our fifth grade. In 2001, the fifth-grade students did not have time to get into fractions. The teachers were spending all of their time reviewing and re-teaching basic computation skills. They never had time to get to fractions. In 2005, the fifth-grade will not only cover fractions, they will use fractions to introduce decimals and percentages. They also started the year with a unit on Algebra. Using "Hands-on Algebra," the students start the year reviewing all the computational skills they have mastered in previous grades. The Algebra unit is a fun unit that ties nicely into the application of skills. They will also teach a major unit in geometry and measurement. This is now possible because students are coming to the fifth grade much better prepared. The time for reviewing and re-teaching has essentially been eliminated, giving the teacher up to nine weeks of time to use for new instruction.

Our typing program is another example of how data has helped us use time differently. Originally, we introduced keyboarding in the fourth grade. As students became more proficient at using technology, introduction was moved to the second semester of third grade. As first and second-grade students started using the keyboarding program as a free-time activity, we were able to move introduction to the start of third grade. The time saved at the fourth-grade and fifth-grade levels is now used for the application of keyboarding, with these students typing their assignments instead of writing them. I am often asked which keyboarding program we are using. The more interesting question is, "Why are we using this particular program?"

## Student Involvement

When we first got the lab in place, I needed to purchase a keyboarding program for the students. I ordered all the keyboarding programs that were site licensed that I could find. I wanted a site license so that I could easily access the data on how all the students were doing. At that time, there were six programs that were able to be site based and that said they were for the elementary. I ordered a copy of all six of them and then asked six, top fifth-grade students to evaluate each program. After each fifth grader had spent at least one hour on each program, they evaluated the programs.

When all six had used each program, I asked them to recommend the one for the school to purchase. They recommended "All the Right Type," and we have been using it ever since. The kids really like it and, even better, the program does teach them to keyboard. On another level, the students were becoming active participants in academic decisions that affected their learning, and this buy-in transferred to all academic areas.

As we know, learning is incremental. For instance, once a student can show mastery of the keyboard, the student is allowed and encouraged to use that skill. This concept should apply to all learning. However, when all students have to learn the same things everyday until the class is ready to move on, time is a constant and learning a variable. When students are taught what they need to know and not what they already know, time is the variable, and learning becomes the constant.

# 3

# DEVELOPING AN AT-RISK PROGRAM

A strong at-risk program is the safety net that allows students to take risks without fear of failure, allows teachers to raise expectations, and gives parents the reason to support higher expectations from the staff.

Westside's at-risk plan was developed by a group of parents and teachers. It purposely utilizes language from the Wyoming Department of Education and the U.S. Department of Education. This allows Westside to use our at-risk plan to fulfill many of the state and federal requirements. It also helps with grant writing, parent communication, and completing required reports. A full copy of the at-risk plan is in appendix A.

## Developing an After-School Study Program

The real power of our plan is the after-school programs. There are essentially two after-school programs that run concurrently for sixty minutes each, Monday through Thursday. The first line of help is our homework/study program. We provide a safe, quiet area for students to work on their homework or study. One staff member supervises the area and will provide help as time allows. Students can self-select the study program, or teachers can recommend and request that students attend. Students use this time to finish or get caught up with their homework.

We have divided homework into two categories: work that did not get done during the school day, and work that is designed to be done at home to extend practice time. The after-school homework program allows students to use the time to complete any homework. Students that do not use their class time efficiently can use the after-school time to complete their assignments. This is a quiet, supervised time. It is not intended as a situation where a tutor will give extra help. The teacher will also assign this time to students who have not completed assignments within the assigned time frame, which provides motivation to students to use their school time efficiently. Some parents and students also request the after-school time to complete assigned practice work intended for homework. Parents really appreciate this program, especially those that work late. When the parent gets home, they can be a parent, instead of fighting with their child over homework. The parent generally becomes very supportive of the school.

We have seen several positive changes due to the after-school homework/study program. Homework is tied to standards. The parents and students know what our standards are, and they see the tie between the work and meeting the requirements for that grade. This program reinforces the need for students to meet all the standards. It also helps some parents avoid a conflict with their child in completing homework since it is all done at school.

> The At-Risk Program allows teachers to raise their expectations.

In addition, the student no longer has an excuse for not completing homework. They know, even in the first grade, that they have to finish their work. If they don't get it done during the day, then they will spend an hour of their time to complete it. Students really do learn to be responsible for completing their work. My fifth-grade teachers used to really complain about students not getting their work done. While it still happens, it is the exception, instead of the rule. The first couple of years that we used this program, we would often have up to twenty students a night doing homework. Today, we seldom have more than five or six, even though the student's workload has dramatically increased.

Another benefit of this program has been increased staff expectations. Prior to the homework program, teachers were hesitant to assign homework because they knew it would be a struggle to get the students to complete the assignments. The slower students in the class often set the pace for the whole class. The homework program has given the teachers the support they needed to ensure that all the students would complete their work. They do not have to lower their expectations because of a few students who are not willing to work. The program has also given the teachers more time because they do not have to continually fight with students to turn in their work, make new copies of worksheets, or contact parents because the work is not getting done.

# Using an After-School Tutor Program

Our second after-school program is our tutor program, which is standards-driven. Students can only access it by teacher request. Our Title I teacher is in charge of the tutor program with up to five tutors that can be used each night. Students are assigned to this program by teacher referral. A student may be referred to this program after the classroom teacher has provided initial instruction and at least one remediation cycle on a skill. If the student cannot show mastery on that standard or skill, a tutor referral is appropriate. The classroom teacher is also responsible for contacting the parent to explain the problem and to let the parent know to pick-up the child after the tutor session. The referral states the standard/skill and how it was taught in the classroom. The Title I teacher assigns the student to a tutor and helps the tutor plan lessons, locate materials, and develop an instructional plan to use with the student. Tutoring is generally one-on-one. At times, if two or three students are deficient in the same skill or standard, the tutor will work with all three. The student is dismissed from the program as soon as mastery of the skill is demonstrated.

Occasionally, a student has a great amount of difficulty mastering a standard or skill. In these cases, we will dismiss the student from the after-school tutoring program for a few days or weeks. After this period of time, the student is put back into the tutor program with a different tutor who provides instruction in a different manner. We have found that occasionally a student really needs time away from the skill. This also gives the student a different way of looking at the problem and, hopefully, a different approach to the solution.

The tutor program has several benefits. The students see it as a help, not a punishment. The focus is on learning a specific standard or skill. It has really helped the students see the need for paying attention and working hard during the school day. Students know they have to learn what is being taught. The student can use school time or they can use their time, but they will learn the standards and skills.

# Summer School Provides Additional Time

Summer school is an important part of our at-risk program. It is essentially an extension of our tutor program and an option for some parents. It is designed to give students more time to master the standards, and there is not a cost to the parents. It is the last way the school can give extra time and help to students to master the standards before retention.

Summer school is divided into two, three-week sessions. Students working on mastery of standards only attend until the standards are mastered. All three elementary schools in Powell send students to the same summer school. There is a teacher and an aide for each grade level as well as a lab manager, a librarian, and an administrator. Summer school runs form 8:30 to 11:30, Monday through Friday.

Six years ago, summer school had around twenty students from each grade level, assigned to summer school to master specific standards. Failure to attend would result in retention. Last year, each grade level had about sixteen students, with only two or three working on mastery of standards. The rest of the students were there to maintain the skills that had given them trouble during the school year.

The maintenance program began as fewer and fewer students were required to attend summer school. Students that had a lot of trouble passing a standard in reading or math were recommended to attend at least one session of summer school. This idea is sold to parents as a maintenance program to help the student maintain mastery and be able to use those skills next year. Those students who were in the after-school tutor program or who required lots of extra help to master reading and math standards are recommended for summer school. Teachers ask the parents to send those students; it is not required. The extra time during the summer helps the student retain those skills that were hard to master and cuts down on the amount of review required in the fall.

The Westside at-risk program is purposely set up in levels. The goal is to give support where it is needed. The at-risk program allows the teacher to have higher expectations, cover more curriculum and engage all students in learning. Some students require lots of support; some do not need any. By setting the program in steps, it does not waste students' time and allows us to focus our resources where they are most needed.

## Parents Are More Supportive

Parents are more supportive of our expectations because we are helping ensure that all students master the standards and skills. I have really tried to communicate to parents that we will do everything we can to help students master our standards. I make sure that parents know that I budget money for the after-school programs; money that could be used for library books, textbooks, computer hardware, etc. This helps put value on the programs and tells parents that the staff and I feel the programs are important.

The school board has also made learning important. They adopted a policy that requires all students to master the standards. Failure to demonstrate mastery can result in retention upon the discretion of the building principal. This gave me a lot of leverage with parents. We always give parents a choice. They can support the after-school programs, have their child go to summer school or have their child retained. The choice isn't whether the child will master the standards; it is how and when.

Teachers have been able to raise their expectations because of the after-school tutor program. The teachers will teach a standard and assess it. The students who do not pass will receive at least one remediation, if not a couple, by the teacher. After the re-teaching, there are usually one or two students who are not able to demonstrate mastery. Those students are moved into the tutor program. This allows the teacher to continue through the curriculum with the whole class, knowing that the student who did not pass will get one-on-one instruction and will pass the standard. Class time involves the whole class and focuses on new material. There is very little class time wasted because the teacher has to resort to small re-teaching groups during the school day.

The tutor program has gone from ten to twelve students a night to five or six a night. With the focus on all students mastering all the standards, the students, parents, and teachers have bought into the idea that all kids can learn, and we will ensure that they do learn. The tutor program is not a punishment for not learning; it is an extra help so that all can learn.

# 4

# USING DATA TO FOCUS INSTRUCTION

During 2003, it seemed like every article spoke about the use of data by the school district central office to help schools improve. What they were really saying was that the data gave central office the ability to put pressure on a school to improve. Of course, central office readily told principals what they needed to do to improve test scores. However, wails of indignation would go up from central office when the state would use the same data to tell the district that they needed to improve. I am not sure that the officials at central office ever saw the irony.

## Two Types of Data

There are essentially two types of data. The data most people are familiar with is building-level data or summative data, which is used by the U.S. Department of Education and State Department of Education to tell if districts and buildings are being successful. Building-level data generally shows the average percentile that the students at a grade level or classroom level are scoring. It is most often used for comparing classrooms, grade levels, and building achievement over time. At best, it can show trends over time. The other type of data is classroom-level data. Classroom data is formative. It is generally generated by the use of computerized assessments and teacher assessments. This data is often referred to as "screening" data or data for progress monitoring. Computer generated means the teacher did not make the assessment or score the assessment; it is done on and by the computer. Classroom-level data is detailed enough to allow the teacher to make instructional decisions for individual students.

For years, I developed graphs using building-level data. This type of data is basically grade-level averages. Using this data, I can compare different groups and spot trends over time. We now refer to this as disaggregated data. By disaggregating the grade-level averages, I can tell if my boys are doing better than the girls or if Title I students are succeeding as well as the non-Title I students. I can compare the achievement of my special education population to the non-special education population. I also look at how economic groups compare and the differences between the ethnic groups. One year, I compared groups based on the mother's education level. It really was no surprise that the students whose mothers were more educated did better in school than those with less education. As with most of the comparisons, it gave me interesting information; but as the building principal, I was never really sure what to do with it other than try to give more instruction to the students scoring below the average. I realize the need for this data; it provides easily interpreted information on how a building is doing. It is like taking your temperature. It tells you if something is wrong but not how to fix it.

To get a clearer picture of what is wrong, you can put summative data into quartiles. By putting the data into quartiles, instead of just averages, it can be more useful in monitoring growth. Growth is measured as the movement of students from the lower two quartiles into the top two quartiles. Unfortunately, even using quartiles, this type of data is too gross a measurement for making important instructional decisions on individual students. This type of data tells you the student is low, but not why he or she is low.

## Formative Data Leads to Real Improvement

Real, meaningful school improvement comes at the school level, classroom by classroom, not at the district level. This leads to the second type of data, classroom-level or formative data. Formative data is data which shows what skills a student knows and does not know. It is one of the main tools leading to real school improvement. I am often asked what kind of data Westside uses. I usually respond by saying that we use any data that helps the teacher make specific decisions about what a child knows or does not know.

For years, Westside's main data was building-level data. We would use the end-of-year, grade-level averages from the norm-referenced test. That data would tell the teacher, in very broad terms, which students needed additional help in reading or math. The interesting thing was that the teacher already knew who her top and bottom students were; the data just substantiated it. The main intervention was to give those low students extra help or time through the Title I program. Title I students were sent to a different room to receive extra help in reading or math, but they would miss what was being taught in their regular classroom. The Title I program provided enough support to help the students maintain, but it very seldom provided enough help so that the student could exit Title I. The data from the norm-referenced test allowed the student to enter Title I for the extra help, but it did not help the teacher identify what the student did or did not know. This is the way most schools use norm-referenced test data to help individual students.

About the time Westside began using the Accelerated Reading program, I found I could order an item analysis of the Terra Nova results. The item analysis provided the classroom teacher and the Title I teacher with better information on what the student knew and did not know. Using the item analysis, the Title I teacher was able to identify specific skills (items missed on the test) in which the student was weak. The Title I program changed from supporting what was being done in the regular classroom to teaching those skills in which the student was weak. Once the skills were identified, the teacher provided instruction in those specific areas. The Title I teacher was using the data to change what was being taught to each student. Students started to exit Title I as they got caught up with their skills and began scoring higher on the Terra Nova norm-referenced test.

## Time and Structure as Obstacles to Learning

Using the success the Title I teacher was having, I tried to get the classroom teachers to use the norm-referenced data in their classrooms. I found that even if the teacher was willing to use the data, the daily school structure actually prevented the data from being used effectively. Time and structure were the two main obstacles for the classroom teacher. What did the teacher do with the kids who knew the skill while working with students who did not know the skill? Another major problem was how the teacher found time to remediate while still teaching all the new material. Centers were used to some success; but test scores, moving students from the bottom two quartiles to the top two quartiles, really did not change. Individual scores did improve, but class averages remained the same.

## Formative Data from a Computer

Another tool for collecting data came unexpectedly. Westside was given the Jostens learning lab, now called the Compass/Odyssey program. It had been sitting in the middle school, unused, for a couple of years. It was a Mac server running the Compass/Odyssey program and five Mac LC computers. It was the best gift Westside ever received.

The Compass/Odyssey program did two things; it tested students at grade level in reading, math, and language arts and gave an itemized report by skill on what the students knew and did not know. It also provided instruction on any of the areas tested. The skills being assessed were aligned to the skills being tested on most nationally normed tests.

It allowed us to assess students at grade level in focused areas. For example, a student would take the fifteen to thirty-minute assessment on affixes at their grade level. We would get an immediate printout on what skills the student knew or did not know, aligned to the major norm-referenced tests.

> By focusing instruction on specific skills, students could make great gains.

Using the Compass/Odyssey program in our Title I program, we could quickly develop an individualized reading plan or math plan for every Title I student. By using the data from the Compass/Odyssey program to really focus our teaching on what the students needed, we were able to help many of the Title I students make more than a year's gain in a year. We started to actually exit more students than we were qualifying.

Identifying holes, skills not mastered in a student's reading and math background, and then teaching to those skills were leading to students becoming more successful. That success was apparent in their daily work and on their norm-referenced tests. It was also clear that the students retained these skills because they were continually using them for solving higher level applications. The success of using formative data in the Title I program led us to look for additional ways to get data for the classroom.

## Formative Data for Screening

We started to look for additional computer programs that would give us quick formative data to help individualize instruction. We wanted assessments that would act as a screening tool in reading and math. We purchased the computerized STAR Reading program to use in second through fifth grade to determine a student's beginning reading level and to keep track of growth in reading during the year.

After using the STAR Reading for awhile, we also purchased the STAR Math and STAR Early Literacy. These assessments are given up to three times a year in one of our computer labs. Each takes about fifteen minutes. The data is used in two ways: first, as summative data, providing beginning and end-of-year averages to show growth for state and federal reports; and second, as formative data to help put students into flexible action groups and for identifying areas for whole group instruction. We also use the data to show parents, students and teachers the growth that has taken place.

All students are assessed at the beginning of the school year. I ask that they are assessed again in January so the teachers can monitor the progress they are making. At the end of the year, they are assessed again so we can measure the growth. This report is shared with the student and with their parents. The STAR Early Literacy is only given in the first and second grade. Once the student is reading at a second-grade level, they start taking the STAR Reading test. STAR Math is given to second through fifth grade.

Data is now a tool that helps all teachers decide what to teach. When you know where you are going, with standards and benchmarks, the data tells you which road to follow. Data is a tool used to monitor and adjust instruction based on what students need to know and what they are learning. It tells the teacher which student needs more time on a specific skill and which students are ready for enrichment. When a teacher starts to look at formative data, they really can start to differentiate their classroom.

# 5

# USING FLEXIBLE ACTION GROUPING TO REMEDIATE AND ENRICH

Flexible action grouping is a structure change. It was developed as a way to give the staff time to teach specific skills to students needing remediation without holding the rest of the class back. It was an effort to give all students the same instructional advantage our Title I students were getting, instruction based on data.

## Title I Focuses on Weak or Missing Skills

Our Title I program had historically been used to support the classroom teacher. It was basically a tutor program. Working with the Title I teacher, we changed the program to a remediation of the skills that a student was weak in or did not possess. In some cases, those skills were two or three grade levels below where the student was currently placed. The Title I teacher, using data from the computerized Compass/Odyssey program, developed a program specific to each student. The Compass/Odyssey program gave the Title I teacher a printout of the reading and math skills the student had not mastered. The Title I teacher would then develop a folder for each student outlining the skills the student would be taught while in Title I. I supported this change by telling the staff that the time students spent in Title I would be used to "fill holes" in the student's learning. The Title I teacher would no longer support what was happening in the classroom. This was a real change for the staff and required several staff meetings to develop an understanding why it was necessary. It helped that the staff started to see more and more students exiting the Title I program because they no longer qualified.

The Title I teacher and I often discussed the use of data and additional time to help students learn specific skills. The need to "fill holes" in their learning so the student could be successful with later learning was developing into a solid concept. After using this strategy for a couple of years, it was clear that this process really worked. I wanted to move this process of using data, grouping and teaching identified skills into the classroom. The opportunity arose when the third grade started to use the Reading Renaissance program. The Reading Renaissance program is basically 30 to 45 minutes a day of silent reading where the teacher closely monitors what level the books are for each student and how they are doing on their comprehension. Students are tested on their comprehension for each book they read. To spend this amount of time silent reading, the teachers needed a way to spend less time on remediation.

## Moving Title I Philosophy into the Classroom

Our screening data showed that the third-grade students were doing very well with basic comprehension, but many students needed more instruction in basic reading skills and language skills. It also showed that all the students would benefit from additional instruction in developing higher-level comprehension strategies.

I approached the two, third-grade teachers with the idea of using our Title I Compass/Odyssey program with all their students to help identify the skills on which students needed to spend more time. They agreed to the concept, so all of the third-grade students were assessed in reading and math using the Compass/Odyssey program. When we went over the data from the assessments, results indicated that most of the students needed some remediation. Using the data, we could easily identify groups of students needing some skills while other groups needed different skills, and the data showed that students could be grouped based on specific skills needing remediation. The problem that became clear was that there were at least four or five different groups. The two classroom teachers could not work effectively with four or five groups of students at the same time, and I did not want to put students into centers or "individualize" instruction. Each group of students needed an instructor so the time spent on remediation would help all students. This problem was solved by assigning a Title I teacher and an aide to the third grade for thirty minutes a day to help with their grouping. Flexible action grouping was born. Flexible action grouping was not to take the place of daily whole group instruction. It was an additional time for remediation, practice, and enrichment.

# Focused Direct Instruction

Flexible action grouping is a thirty-minute session of direct instruction focused on a specific skill requiring remediation as identified by an assessment. Students are put into groups for a four-week to six-week cycle based on the assessment data. At the end of the four-week to six-week cycle the groups are changed, based on the assessment data. The daily schedule for the school was changed to allow the Title I staff to work with each grade level for thirty-minutes a day on reading and a different thirty-minute period for math.

All the students from a grade level are put into small groups, and each group is assigned to a team member. This allows for a ratio of from four to fifteen students per adult in each group. The number of students in a group is determined by the skill being taught. Sometimes, because of the complexity of the skill, large groups are broken into two smaller groups. If everyone needs the same skill, it becomes a whole group unit during whole group instruction time.

Planning is essential, and when it is time for a team to plan for the next cycle, a substitute teacher is provided for each team member for one-half day. The team takes one-half day and reviews the data, puts students into instructional groups based on the data, and develops basic lesson plans for each group. The size of the group varies depending on the skill(s) that need remediation and the number of students needing remediation on that skill.

As the teachers started planning, I bought tubs for hanging files, and the teachers developed files for each skill they taught. This was a little more work to start with, but it has saved a tremendous amount of time over the past few years. The third-grade teachers now have several tubs of files, and when they need a unit on "cause and effect" or for teaching "volume," they just pull out that file. The files are not static. Material is constantly being updated and added to them.

When the teachers attend a workshop on "teaching hands-on fractions," a new file is developed using new ideas. These files have helped the teachers become more aware of what needs to be taught, and the files have given them more control over what is being taught. Instead of a textbook being the curriculum, the teacher is making those decisions based on mastery of standards. This is covered more fully in Chapter 6, *Focusing on Standards and Benchmarks.*

# Data Becomes the Guide

Data comes from many sources. The overriding focus is on a student's mastery of the state standards and the prerequisite skills needed for that mastery. The Compass/Odyssey tests of basic skills, item analysis from the Terra Nova test results, Lexia Quick Reading assessment, and computerized testing like STAR Reading, STAR Math, and STAR Early Literacy are all used to help decide what a student knows and does not know. The use of technology, detailed in Chapter 7, *Making Technology a Tool*, has made data more usable and more available to the staff than ever before. Flexible action grouping utilizes technology as an assessment tool, one that saves teachers' time and allows them to meet individual student needs in a manner not possible even ten years ago.

## Whole Group Instruction

Traditional whole group instruction by the classroom teacher continues to take place each day during a forty-five-minute to sixty-minute period as scheduled by the teacher. Whole group instruction time is used for introducing new skills and concepts to the entire class and to work on application using skills everyone has mastered.

After third grade had used flexible action grouping in reading for one year, we evaluated the results using Terra Nova scores and a survey of the students. The teaching team, two third-grade teachers, a Title I teacher, and an aide, were sold on the program. Test scores had improved dramatically, not only the average percentile, but also the number of students above the first and second quartile. The students indicated that they really liked the grouping. The students liked moving to a new group and focusing on learning in the small group. The teachers were excited about the grouping because they were feeling more successful with their teaching.

## Change Is Difficult

I was excited about the program. From my perspective, I felt that the students, the staff, and I were really changing. The teachers were making decisions based on individual needs, they were collaborating, and they were researching new ways to provide instruction. The students were becoming more successful, they were beginning to understand why they were in school, they had more control of their own learning, and they were having more fun. I just knew that the rest of the staff would be excited. At the end-of-the-year staff meeting, I shared our "new" program and the achievement data with the staff. The idea was to start using flexible action grouping building-wide the next fall. As I outlined the program, I quickly realized that my enthusiasm was not shared by all the staff.

One of the biggest objections centered on trust, although it was not directly stated. What was said was, "I am responsible for the achievement of my students; I can't give up 30 minutes of daily instructional time." I asked a fifth-grade teacher to stand and then asked the other fifth-grade teacher if she thought her co-teacher could teach "cause and effect" to fifth-grade students. The response was "yes." I then asked the Title I teacher and Special Education teacher to stand and asked the rest of the staff if they would trust these two teachers to teach "cause and effect" to their students. Everyone said "yes." Asking those two to sit, I said, "It sounds like you trust each other to teach specific skills. That is all flexible action grouping does. Instead of you teaching the skills by yourself, you now have help. From our building data, it is clear that if we continue using the school day the way we always have we will not be successful with all students. We need to make a structural change." I said that the next fall we would all start using flexible action grouping in reading and math. The rest of the meeting was used to develop the schedule for the next year.

## Scheduling Is a Structural Change

The next hurdle was developing a schedule that would facilitate the flexible action grouping. Building on the idea that "what gets measured gets taught," I built the new schedule around the flexible grouping. I first divided the day into fifteen-minute slots, including time for recess and lunch. To give more time in the morning, I pushed lunch back fifteen minutes. Next came the grouping time. Each grade was given two, fifteen-minute slots in the morning for reading and two, fifteen-minute slots in the afternoon for math. Westside has two Title I staff members, so I scheduled one with each group and one to work in the Title I room with Title I students. Westside also has two special education teachers. Looking at their caseloads and the number of students in each grade, I scheduled both of them into at least one grade level for flexible action grouping. As it worked out, both special education teachers were able to work with two flexible groups in either math or reading. I then worked with the teachers to add in their Title I time, their special education time, physical education (twice a week), music (twice a week), computer lab time (ninety minutes a week) and library time (thirty minutes a week). The only things that could not be changed were the flexible action group times.

We spent about three weeks developing the new schedule. It required a lot of give and take between teachers of the specials. The time and Special Education teacher had to build her time slots in Title I instead of building her schedule around grade levels and the teachers. The biggest change was Title I time. Now, the classroom schedule around the open of the Title I teacher building the classroom teacher.

> The schedule was built around the needs of our students.

What we actually did by building the schedule this way was say that the students requiring extra help are important and that we would first decide when they should get help, instead of just fitting them into a schedule when it was convenient.

## Unexpected Results

That fall, using test results from the previous spring, we all started flexible action grouping. Several staff members were still unhappy about the change but started using it anyway. Just before Christmas break, while I was working at my desk, one teacher, who had been very vocal against the grouping, stormed into my office. She basically kicked the door closed and threw some books onto the corner of my desk. Pointing a finger at me, she said, "Look, I still don't like this grouping but don't change it." She picked up her books and left before I could respond. At that moment, I knew we had turned the corner. Later, I realized we had moved to a category three school in student achievement, as discussed in the Chapter 6, *Focusing on Standards and Benchmarks*. Flexible action grouping was started as a way to improve student achievement. As all the teachers started using data to focus instruction on individual students, the staff and I started to see more and more positive reasons for continuing it.

Another benefit, besides increased student achievement, was the collaboration that was taking place. Using data and giving the team a half-day to organize and plan for each cycle was changing how everyone worked together. That first year I would often sit in on their planning sessions. I enjoyed the discussions that took place as the teachers discussed the data, put students into homogenous groups, decided how long to teach each skill and how to best teach the skill. The sharing of teaching ideas, materials, and insights into how individual students learn really brought the staff together. It also challenged every teacher to do their best.

The Title I teacher and, to a large extent, the special education teacher were quickly becoming experts in our reading and math curriculum. They planned with each grade level. They started sharing the expectations for the next grade and what the previous grade had actually taught the students. Everyone was starting to see beyond their classroom. The staff was beginning to see the bigger picture, which led to higher expectations. Part of the increased expectations came from asking the group teams to rotate who taught certain skills. The Title I and special education teacher had to teach an enrichment group sometime during the year.

# Success Breeds Success

During that first year, every staff member made essentially the same comment to me about the grouping, "I am really having fun doing this." I believe they felt this way because every teacher was being successful and teachers were working together as a team. The teachers were seeing the students succeed. Using data to focus instruction in small groups allowed the teacher to see the "lights" being turned on for each student. The direct instruction, immediate feedback, and thirty-minute time block helped the students be successful. That success built confidence which built more success, and the teachers could see this happening in the students. We all went into teaching to help students. Grouping gave teachers the positive feedback that is often lost in a classroom of twenty or more students. Another positive outcome was the collaboration that was taking place. Teaching has always been an isolated occupation. For the most part, teachers would enter their classroom in September, close the door, and then emerge in May to go home for the summer. The planning time, given every four to six weeks for the flexible action grouping, became an easy way to develop learning communities.

The new schedule changed the focus for the whole day. It forced the classroom teachers in each grade level to work more closely together. It actually required all the teachers at a grade level to maintain the same pacing, keep on the same subject, and not deviate from the reading and math curriculum.

The flexible action grouping required the classroom teachers to follow the same curriculum for whole group instruction. The teachers had to stay together on what was being taught. This has led to even more collaboration and sharing. The teachers are actually sharing ideas that work and do not work. They share materials, and they plan for whole group instruction together. They are even using the same assessments for their units of instruction.

These changes have come about because the teachers saw the value of the flexible action grouping the first year. The first couple of cycles were designed around remediation from the previous year. The rest of the year, the cycles were designed around remediation of what was taught in the whole group instruction.

# Remediation and Enrichment

The second year, flexible action grouping brought even more surprises. We did not expect it, but during the second year, a real problem developed: what to do with the students who did not need any remediation. We felt we needed to continue with the grouping; it was working. We did not want to waste student's time teaching them what they already knew, and we did not want to accelerate their learning by putting them into the next curriculum level. We decided to start teaching the application of those skills already mastered. How this was handled is discussed more fully in Chapter 8, *Providing Enrichment.*

I believe that Westside, with two teachers at each grade level, is an optimum size for flexible action grouping. Larger schools that have visited Westside to get ideas for school improvement have adapted flexible action grouping to their situation. A school with four classrooms at each grade level started grouping with just two of the classrooms. They plan on combining the four classrooms after working with the management for a year. A school with seven classrooms at each grade level has two teachers that really want to do the grouping, so they are piloting the program. A school with five classrooms at each grade level has organized its schedule by putting two classrooms in one time slot and three in another. The important thing that is happening in all of these schools is that the staffs are starting to look at what skills a student does not know and develop a way to remediate those skills without wasting the time of those students who already know it. Using data, they are all finding ways to identify time to work together and plan as a team.

# 6

# FOCUSING ON STANDARDS AND BENCHMARKS

Student achievement is tied to many factors: home, intelligence, motivation, curriculum, expectations, instruction, and learning styles to name just a few. Of these areas, curriculum is often the area that receives the most attention and change, yet it often provides the smallest increase in student achievement. Curriculum is what is being taught; however, in many districts and schools, it is confused with what textbook or what materials are being used. In fact, in many schools, the curriculum is the textbook or the program being used.

Being the principal of my own elementary school for over twenty years, combined with the excellent resources available in Wyoming, has allowed me to try many different programs and textbooks, including several basal series. Basal series were introduced to "help" teachers do a better job in the classroom. This was because many states had low standards for teacher training, and a strong basal helped overcome the weaknesses of the instructor. Instead of the teacher making curriculum decisions, the basal became the curriculum. Administrators could monitor the instruction by seeing what page the teacher was on in the basal. Some states are even requiring that all teachers teach from the same page in the basal at the same time.

However, utilizing a basal series will not raise student achievement substantially. Several approaches to curriculum delivery that are more effective are discussed later in this chapter. In addition to how schools deliver the curriculum, I have found that the other primary factors that contribute to the quality of student achievement are the use of technology and assessment data, teacher collaboration, type of enrichment, and parent involvement. Examination of these factors has enabled me to put schools into four categories based on average student achievement.

## Category One

Each category can be measured by the academic progress of the students. The category a school falls into is identified by the students' average test scores on a norm-referenced test. Category one schools have averages between the 30th and the 60th percentile, and the curriculum is primarily delivered from a canned program or a textbook which is required for all grade levels and teachers. In many schools, teachers are even required to teach from the same page on the same day. Assessment data is used to determine grades but not to determine if a student has mastered the material. Some students may get extra reading or math time, but it is at the expense of missed classroom time. Instruction for students needing help tends to be more of the same, and there is little use of technology, especially technology tied to specific skills. Instruction tends to be lecture and worksheets with very little collaboration between teachers. Enrichment tends to be more of the same or "free" reading time. Parents do not feel welcome in the classroom, and they are not an active part of the educational process.

## Category Two

A category two school has students scoring on average in the 50th to 70th percentile on a national norm-referenced test. Some students may be receiving extra time in before-school and after-school programs or during a session of summer school. The primary use of assessment data is to give grades, but it is also starting to be used at the building level to identify subgroups in need of more instruction. There are adopted texts at grade level, but teachers use additional, supplemental materials to individualize instruction. It is not a page-by-page approach, and standards are starting to replace textbooks. There is some use of technology, but it is not aligned to specific individual needs. A hands-on approach, centers, collaborative learning, and project learning are being used sporadically in the classroom. Enrichment is organized, but time is not usually allocated to the enrichment activities, and the activities are not tied to the application of skills already mastered. There is some collaboration between teachers at grade level. Parents are encouraged to support school but are not an active part of what is happening in the school. In order for a school to move from category two to category three, a paradigm shift must take place in how the staff thinks about education.

## Category Three

A category three school has students scoring on average in the 70th to 90th percentile on a national norm-referenced test. The curriculum is standards-driven at all grade levels, and there is clear articulation of what is expected of all students at each grade level. Time is a variable for students, and the amount of time a student spends on a standard is determined by how quickly he/she can show mastery of the standard. There is flexibility of time before, after, and during the school day. Instruction is tied to what the students are learning, and the variety of instructional approaches is noticeable. Textbooks and supplemental materials are used by the teacher to teach the standards, and the teacher selects those materials that best meet the needs of her/his students to learn the standards. Assessment of the standards and benchmarks is ongoing to ensure mastery by all students, and data is used to determine if the student needs more or less time on a standard. Technology is used by the teacher and the student as a teaching and learning tool to provide data for decision making, to remediate, to provide practice, and to provide enrichment, all tied to standards. Collaboration is planned and ongoing at and across grade levels. Enrichment, which is tied to the application of skills, is given time during and after the school day. It is planned and used to help keep students engaged in the learning process. Parents are encouraged to be part of the school, and there are specific plans used to get and keep parents involved with the school.

## Category Four

A category four school has students scoring, on average, in the 80th to 99th percentile on a national norm-referenced test. The curriculum is totally standards-driven with the primary grades focusing on basic skills in reading, math, and writing, so the intermediate grades can focus on the application of those skills. Technology is fully integrated into the learning process, and teachers tend to be facilitators in the learning process. The system or school structure can change quickly to better meet the needs of individual students needing more time (remediation) or enrichment. Collaboration is the norm for the building. Parents are supportive of the idea that all students can learn and that time is a variable. The goal is to have all students master all the standards.

## Changing from One Category to Another

The shift from a category one to a category two school is characterized by changing textbooks, programs, and instructional techniques. The staff, parents, and students are starting to work together.

The shift from a category two to a category three school is a paradigm shift. It requires the school to change its structure. Teachers become facilitators and collaborators, and students become involved in school and are more responsible for their learning. Parents not only understand the need for an education; they support the increased demands placed on their child by the classroom teacher and school. There is the expectation that all students will master the standards and skills at each grade level, so they can start to apply them.

The shift from a category three to a category four school is observable in the flexibility the teacher and school has to make quick changes based on individual needs as identified by data. Students at all grade levels are moving into the application of skills they have already mastered. Instruction has a strong component based on brain-based research and learning styles.

## Today's Schools

Most schools are currently functioning in the first category. They continue to rely on their "curriculum" or the materials/programs they are using to help students achieve. These schools are following the traditional philosophy of one text or one program for all students. A school-wide reading basal, a specific math program, or even an instructional method is mandated for all teachers to use. When all of the students do not achieve at a high level, then the text, program or instructional method is changed.

This type of change is consistent with a category one structure. It usually just changes which group of students are achieving, but overall average achievement does not change. A basal reader that has a strong phonics program will have the analytic learners achieving at a higher rate than the global learners because they work best with a strong structure and sequence. They can learn all the parts before they see the whole picture. Inversely, changing to a basal with a strong whole language approach will have the global learners achieving higher but the achievement of the analytic learners will drop, because the global learn likes to see the whole picture first then add in the parts. They like to see how words are used before learning how to break words apart, like a phonics approach. Today's research on how the brain learns is showing that today's students are split: 60% are analytic learners, and 40% are global learners. When dealing with this type of split in a classroom, a change in what basal is being used will not help class averages. It will just change the group that is achieving the highest. To really get improvement, each group requires a different intervention.

## Standards Become the Curriculum

Westside moved to a category two school when we went to a standards-based model instead of a textbook model. A standards-based model identifies what needs to be taught to mastery for all students. It is based on what a student needs to know to graduate and be successful when entering college. From those standards, benchmarks are identified. The benchmarks are those skills that are needed to show mastery of the standard. The curriculum was then mapped backward from twelfth grade to kindergarten. This gave a curriculum map for each grade level that the teacher could follow. It identified those benchmarks and standards necessary for students to be successful at the next grade level and made the basic assumption that curriculum must be sequential. The benchmarks or skills a kindergartner masters were built upon in the first grade. Those skills were built upon in the second grade and so forth. The district also built assessments to determine if the student had mastered the benchmarks identified at each grade level.

Once the sequence of benchmarks had been identified and the assessments developed, the teachers were asked to ensure that all students mastered all the skills for their grade level. Mastery of all the standards became the primary goal for all teachers.

The teachers at Westside do not use a basal text for any of the subject areas. They use a variety of texts and materials to ensure that all students master the identified skills. The texts are aligned to individual student needs. The teacher is making instructional decisions based on what the student needs so he/she can best learn the required material.

## Clear Standards and Benchmarks Required

The testing points out that in the elementary, even more so than the upper grades, students must learn the basics before they can be taught how to apply those basic skills. At the elementary level, a very clear set of standards, skills and benchmarks must be established so educators can be held accountable for teaching them and students held accountable for learning them.

The ability to apply skills or "think" comes from a strong skill base. This allows the teacher to teach students

> **Mastery of skills is necessary before application.**

how to transfer skills and concepts from one situation to another. A strong skill base allows the student to take pieces of information from many sources and use it to solve a new problem.

Many programs have been developed to teach application so students can "meet" the new standards. The programs are built on the assumption that by doing a lot of application problems the student will learn how to do application problems. This assumption fails because there is not enough time in the school day to learn the basics through application. A strong foundation in basic facts must be built before the walls of application will stand on their own.

## Becoming a Category Three School

Westside successfully moved to a category three school by changing our structure so we could make time a variable while continuing to focus on standards and benchmarks. In the primary grades, kindergarten through third, many students require the whole day to master the benchmarks or skills, the foundation of all future learning. Those students spend the majority of the day working on those skills. As students show mastery of the skills, they are moved into applications requiring the use of those skills. This is especially true at the fourth and fifth grades. The majority of the fourth and fifth graders spend most of their time on the application of skills: higher-level reading applications, moving into algebra, understanding percentages, and in other words, getting the students to compare, contrast, and apply those skills that were developed in the previous grades.

## Expectations Affect Curriculum

As a category three school we have made many changes to our curriculum and to our expectations. Math is an easy example. At second grade, we expect all students to show mastery on all the basic addition and subtraction math facts. Using Precision Teaching, mastery means passing ninety problems in three minutes with 80% accuracy. If the students do not show mastery by the end of the year, they are required to attend summer school. At third grade, all students have to show mastery of all the basic facts: addition, subtraction, multiplication, and division. Failure to show mastery means the student will attend summer school.

> Students need a strong foundation in the benchmarks before they are asked to apply them.

Several years ago, Westside had a large number of fifth-grade students, ten or eleven out of forty, who were having a very difficult time learning how to do long division, which is an application of basic addition, subtraction, multiplication, and division. I volunteered to help the Title I teachers so that each of us could work with a small group, providing more individual attention and direct instruction. After a week of thirty minutes a day instruction in long division, I was very frustrated. My group was not making progress. I took a few minutes and task analyzed the problem. My students were not making progress because they did not know their basic facts. They did not know the basic addition, subtraction, multiplication and division facts. By the time they "figured" out the facts, they would forget what step they were on in the long division process. I switched to teaching them how to use a calculator to do the basic facts, not the problem. They quickly learned the process of long division.

At our next staff meeting, I related this experience to the staff. The students' ability to apply skills, basic facts, to long division was a major problem. Mastery of basic facts was not a standard or a benchmark, but it was a tool skill that was necessary for almost all future math skills and applications. We require that all students learn the alphabet so they can become readers. We decided that basic facts were to math as the alphabet was to reading. That year, we added mastery of the basic facts to our math standards.

Now, first grade starts the students memorizing the addition facts right away, along with all the other math standards. In addition to the change in thinking about basic facts, we decided that math could and should be taught in two different categories. We now teach basic facts and skills as one area and applications as another. They are two separate areas. The facts are taught each day for a few minutes. Math applications, using the facts, are taught during a different part of the day.

All the staff uses Precision Teaching as an instructional tool. Using several computer programs, it is easy to individualize instruction in basic facts for every student. This same technique is used for teaching tool skills in spelling, reading, language, and writing.

## Basic Facts Critical to Success in Math

The first year we required all students to master their facts, there were six students in the third grade who had to attend summer school. In a couple of cases, it was hard to convince the parents that I would retain the student if summer school was not attended. They did attend; and within three weeks, all six could show mastery of their facts. Since that first year, I have not

> Fluency in basic math facts is the foundation for math applications.

had one student recommended for summer school due to not mastering the basic facts. The concerns the staff had about students not being able to memorize the facts really never developed. This new expectation is accepted by parents because we have been able to show them how important it is.

The Westside staff is now teaching more math skills and more math applications than we thought possible just a few years ago. Now that the students know their facts and understand the idea that the facts are different than math standards, the majority of students are feeling successful in math. They are even enjoying learning how to apply math skills to real-life problems. In our last student survey, 40% of the students identified math as their favorite subject. This shows in our class averages on the norm-referenced Terra Nova testing. All the grades are averaging above the 80th percentile, with several averaging above the 90th percentile in math. We have consistently been one of the top five schools in math on the state fourth-grade assessment.

## Teach Beyond the Standard

Another change in our curriculum (again I'll use math as an example) is teaching above or beyond the standards. Westside uses the district math standards for mastery. To ensure that students can use the skills and applications identified on the district standards, we have developed our own building-level standards which require more than the district does. An example is the second-grade standard for fractions. The district standard requires the students to identify fractions from one-eighth to one-half in an illustration. Our building standard has students adding and subtracting like fractions, knowing the term denominator and numerator, and using fractions in everyday life.

> Teach more than the students need to know to pass the standard.

The second-grade students have fun learning about fractions. The teacher enjoys teaching fractions to the higher level because she only assesses the students on the district standards. This over-teaching ensures that all the students can do well on the district assessment. It also increases the students' confidence in math which motivates them to do more in math. We are pushing students in fractions because we want the fifth-grade students to be able to do and understand percentages so they can use that math skill in reading, science, and social studies at the fifth-grade level.

Last year, I took fifteen, fifth graders to Pizza Hut for a reading party. Each student had earned 150 or more Accelerated Reading points. The students decided to have an eating contest; points were given to every item on the menu, and it was boys against girls. Since there were more girls than boys, they totaled their points for each group, and then figured the percentage that each group made. The boys won. It was very rewarding to watch them apply those math skills to a real situation.

## Students Practice Reading

The other main curriculum area is reading. Westside does not use a reading basal or series. All grades use the library and the Accelerated Reading program along with texts at each grade level. Kindergarten through second grade use guided reading as their primary instructional technique. All grades use Modern Curriculum Press as a phonics book and the Lexia phonics programs on the computer.

The Accelerated Reading program is the practice portion of each grade's reading program. Six years ago, our library's yearly circulation was around 8,000 volumes. Today, our circulation easily exceeds 30,000. This is in a school of 220 students. After determining the reading level of each book and marking the book with the reading level, we purchased comprehension tests on them. After reading a book, the student takes the comprehension test over the material. The test results from the Accelerated Reading program confirm that, not only are the books being read, the students comprehend what they are reading.

Most basal series have a short story for all the students to read. Then, a skill or two is taught, often not related to the story, a couple of worksheets are completed, and the cycle starts over. The students really never have to do a lot of reading or practice the reading skills being taught by the teacher. The Accelerated Reading program motivates the students to practice reading using library books. The students are held accountable for what they are reading because of the computerized comprehension test they take on every book they read.

The teacher teaches the skills identified by the standards during the classroom instructional time. During the Accelerated Reading time, the teacher monitors what the students are reading and works with individuals on fluency and even some skill re-teaching. The teacher ensures that the students are reading books in his/her zone of proximal development, or ZPD, from Renaissance Learning. Research has shown that if a student reads below or above their ZPD, vocabulary development is inhibited. If a student reads in his/her ZPD, vocabulary development is maximized. From working with the Accelerated Reading program for thirteen years, I fully agree with the research.

## Reading Practice Begins in Kindergarten

In 2003, Westside had thirty-nine, fifth-grade students. When they took the Terra Nova norm-referenced test at the end of the year, thirteen of them scored above the twelfth grade on the reading composite score. This type of reading ability is not unusual for Westside since we have become a category three school. In 2005, every kindergarten student had earned at least ten Accelerated Reading points. That means they had "read" at least twenty books and passed the Accelerated Reading comprehension test on each one. Most of the students could not actually read the books, so the books were read to the student, and then the test was read to the student. The student had to answer the questions correctly to earn the points. Of our forty kindergarten students, thirty of them are now reading at a primer level.

When this group of students enter first grade in the fall, they will all have the skill of oral comprehension. They should all have phonemic awareness as a tool for decoding words; and if a few do not, they will receive extra help in phonemic awareness during flexible group time. Some of the students are already reading at a second-grade level. This allows the first-grade teacher to begin whole group instruction at a significantly higher level. With flexible grouping, all the students will be challenged. When a teacher uses data to individualize instruction, students are able to move through the curriculum at their own pace. By teaching to standards and keeping an eye on all the basic skills, the teacher also ensures that all students master all the identified skills.

## Computerized Phonics

While the standards do not directly address phonics, it is an important component of learning to read, and Westside has a strong phonics program. Phonics is taught at all grade levels using Modern Curriculum Press phonics workbook as a guide. To tie into the different learning styles and provide additional practice, all students are also working on the computerized Lexia phonics programs at least three times a week. Lexia makes three phonics programs. "Early Reading," which is for the kindergarten level, is built around research on phonemic awareness and letter-sound recognition. "Phonics Based Reading" is for first through third grade. It moves students from letter-sound recognition to syllables. The third program, Reading S.O.S., Strategies for Older Students, is for third through eighth-grade students. It moves students from syllables through Greek and Latin affixes. These three programs have a very strong research base, work well on a network, and are not very expensive. They are in a very student-friendly format, and each has a strong data component allowing the teacher to monitor progress. I have watched all the students use these programs over the last two years and can highly recommend them. Not only do the students enjoy the programs, they learn from them.

While on a recent field trip with the third grade, one of the presenters asked the kids about hydrothermal activity. The presenter was very impressed when several of the kids could tell him the meaning. All three said they had learned about hydro and thermal at school on the computer. I checked, and both words are covered in Lexia S.O.S.

Other indicators that the programs are working are our word analysis scores on the Terra Nova and overall improvement in reading scores as measured by the STAR Reading assessment. The year before we introduced Lexia, the thirty-nine, second-grade students had an average at the 76th percentile in word analysis on the Terra Nova. As third graders, the same students had an average in word analysis at the 94th percentile on the Terra Nova. The main change in instruction was the addition of Lexia "Phonics Based Reading" in the third grade. The students would spend fifteen minutes, three times a week, working on the program. Using the STAR Reading assessment at the beginning and end of the year, students showed an average gain of ten percentile points. They also showed an average increase in reading level of 1.45 years in .8 of a year.

## Technology is a Necessary Tool

Using technology, in this case the Lexia phonics programs, is an excellent way to extend, remediate, and enrich what is being taught in the classroom. Using technology to extend classroom instruction helps move skills from the short-term to the long-term memory. In the classroom, the primary learning mode is auditory with some visual. On the computer, visual, auditory, and kinesthetic are all combined with the student in control. When good computer programs are tied to the classroom instruction, it produces a high rate of learning without requiring a lot of additional classroom time. The teacher uses the time to monitor and adjust how the students are using the program and what parts of the program they are using.

## Limiting the Curriculum

Westside has adopted the philosophy that students must learn how to read, write, and be proficient in math. In fact, in kindergarten through third grade, we do not give grades in science and social studies. The standards for those areas are covered in our guided reading using nonfiction books.

Several years ago at a staff meeting, I asked the kindergarten through third-grade staff to quit teaching science and social studies. A gasp went up from the staff. The fourth and fifth-grade teachers started asking how they were going to get students to meet the science and social studies standards if those subjects were not taught in the primary grades. I asked them, "If the kids come to you reading at grade level and doing math at grade level, can't you spend more time on those subjects?" They said, "Yes." I then brought out stacks of new books for each grade level, multiple copies of nonfiction books at the appropriate reading level that covered the science and social studies standards for first through third grade. All the new nonfiction books could also be tested using the Accelerated Reading program. Those books became part of the first-grade through third-grade teachers' guided-reading books or just books that students were required to read. Being great teachers, they all made lists of the books and then kept track of each student's reading to ensure that all students had read all the titles and passed the Accelerated Reading test at 80 percent or better on each title.

> Nonfiction books lead to higher achievement.

The teachers didn't actually stop teaching science and social studies; they just made those subjects part of their reading and math units. To ensure that the student was learning the material on a science standard, the teacher would have the student read the corresponding book and test their comprehension on it in the Accelerated Reading program. If the student got 80%, he/she did not have to read the book again and the teacher checked that standard as being met. I believe that students are actually learning more science and social studies now than before. Lessons are more hands-on, the students have more knowledge about the subject, and the students have more fun because the material isn't being "tested." This system also has the teachers and students using technology to save time. The teachers are telling me that the kids are starting to really enjoy reading nonfiction books for the information they contain. I often have first and second graders come up to me and tell me about a new animal they have read about, how a volcano works, or how deep the ocean is. As their general knowledge grows about the world around them, so does their vocabulary, comprehension and ability to process new information.

## Reading Non-Fiction Is Critical

This same model of using nonfiction reading was taken into the fourth and fifth grades. Now, all the staff is using nonfiction books in their teaching of reading. Over the years, my staff and I have attended several workshops on cross-curricular instruction. I find it poetic that we really did not start going cross-curricular until I asked the staff to quit teaching science and social studies.

The fourth-grade and fifth-grade teachers have taken it a step further. They have started requiring the students to read specific curriculum books first, then the teacher teaches the unit over that area. This allows the teacher to be more of a facilitator. The teacher is able to ask the student to do more writing and research and can lead terrific discussions because all the students have a common vocabulary and understanding before the unit begins.

> Integrate science and social studies into reading and math.

Using nonfiction has helped all the students become better at reading and writing and has improved their general knowledge. It is so much easier to teach finding the main idea and details using nonfiction, especially for those middle and low students. Our writing has also improved because the nonfiction reading helps those same students develop a clear picture of how to write using a main idea and supporting details. Their general knowledge or vocabulary improves because they understand the books and find them interesting.

When a school moves away from a basal approach to a standards approach, it empowers the teacher. By identifying the standards and benchmarks, or skills, that all students must master to be proficient, materials are matched to the individual student. A standards approach allows the teacher to actually teach.

# 7

# MAKING TECHNOLOGY A TOOL

In many ways, I have been fortunate to have been a building principal from the time there was not any technology to today, when we are quickly becoming totally dependent on technology. This has given me a perspective that many new principals cannot see and many older principals refuse to see.

When technology first came to Westside, it was the old Apple II. My office used it to keep track of attendance and provide some demographic data for student records. The students used the Apple II to access floppy disks with content-specific programs. After a couple of years, I even ran an after-school enrichment class for fourth-grade and fifth-grade students on how to program in Apple Basic. It was great fun, and the parents loved seeing the programs the students produced. Looking back, I'm not sure it really helped the students academically. The time they spent on the computer did not provide any data to the teacher. The programs they spent time on were not specific to their individual needs. We were using technology because it was the newest and greatest, and we were riding that wave.

## Computer Programs Are Today's Textbooks

As I look at technology today, I see a real need for it. I would even make the analogy that textbooks were to the industrial age what technology is to the communication age. This does not mean that there is not a place for textbooks, rather it means that in many areas technology can and should replace or supplement the traditional textbook.

Looking at technology strictly from the academic side, disregarding the administrative management programs, I see three main ways that Westside has used technology to improve academic achievement. First, technology provides data to be used for individualization; second, technology provides time for the teacher to individualize; and third, it provides remediation, practice and enrichment for skills and applications that have already been taught. As a school, our job is to ensure that all students master the standards identified by the building, district, state, and now the federal government with the National Assessment of Educational Progress testing. The use of technology in schools provides a valuable tool in meeting this goal.

## Technology Provides Assessment Data

Westside uses computerized assessments to determine what students know and do not know in reading and math. This has been a paradigm shift in thinking. While this shift is covered fully in the chapters on Using Data and Flexible Action Grouping, it is worth addressing more fully.

In the industrial age, schools were not especially worried about student learning since the mission was compulsory attendance. In the communication age, we are responsible for all students learning or mastering standards. The data that comes from using technology is an important tool for accomplishing this goal.

Using a program like the STAR Reading program gives the teacher, in about fifteen minutes, data on each student's reading level. Armed with this knowledge, the teacher can no longer just "teach" reading to the whole group. This knowledge pressures the teacher to individualize instruction. Once the teacher knows at what level a student is reading, it is ineffective for the teacher to provide instruction in reading above or below that level. That same data becomes very useful to the building principal in monitoring on-going student achievement. The use of data from a computerized program helps save instructional time and focus learning for all students.

> Instruction should be at the correct level for the student.

Using the data from the STAR Reading program, the teacher and the school have a valuable tool for helping a student become successful. At Westside, we have assigned grade levels to the majority of books in our library. When a student checks out a book, he is encouraged to choose one at his level. This maximizes the student's learning of vocabulary, resulting in a gain of instructional time.

With additional programs, requiring very little time, the teacher can be provided with even more specific data. The Lexia reading programs show teachers exactly which phonics skills a student does or does not have. The Compass/Odyssey program lists all the reading skills as well as all the comprehension skills a student knows and does not know. An item analysis of a norm-referenced test will also identify specific skills a student knows and does not know. This type of data provides the teacher with a clear map to help guide instruction. Instead of just teaching everything to every student, the teacher is able to individualize. Using the data provided by computerized assessment, the teacher can remediate or enrich depending on the needs of each student.

## Computer Versus Teacher Assessments

Computerized assessment is much different than teacher made tests and worksheets. The computer is not biased; it requires all the students to do the same, and it scores based on what the students can actually do. Classroom assessments are always suspect. Students are experts at playing the game called school.

When I was a teacher, long before electronic grade books were around, I took lots of grades. I wanted my students to be successful, so I reasoned that lots of grades would give me a better picture of what the students knew. Every year, when I figured up the quarter grades, I was always surprised by one or two students in the room. I thought they were doing well, but their grades proved otherwise. They were always raising their hands, answering questions, and turning in the worksheets. The poor grades came because of the occasional tests. The grades that really mattered, assessments of skills, got lost in the day-to-day grades taken on practice work. Teachers are still fooled by students playing the game. The computer measures what a student knows and does not know. It does it quickly and easily and gives the data to the teacher at the press of a button.

## Intuition Is Not Data Driven

As we transitioned to using computerized data, it was difficult for many staff members to let go of their "intuition" and trust the printout. Often the teacher would just "know" that the student could do better or wondered how they did that well. In most cases, I would just have the student retake the assessment. Occasionally, the student would do better or worse; but usually, the same score came up again. In some cases, I would compare the computerized score to the student's norm-referenced score, and we would usually find them the same. At that point, the staff started to believe the printout. Another main use of technology is to give the teachers and students more time. Time is again covered more completely in Chapter 2, *Making Time a Variable*, but it is appropriate to explain how technology gives time to the teacher and student.

# Technology and Time

In the industrial age, time was not a big concern. The elementary teacher had to prepare one math lesson for her class. If she was really good, she would make a few notes about re-teaching some of the students before moving on to the next page in the math book. In the communication age, the goal is to make sure that all students to master all the standards. To achieve this goal, teachers have to individualize their instruction. They cannot go from the first page to the last page of the textbook and expect all students to be there with them. This individualization of lessons takes a lot of time: time to prepare lessons, time to teach each student, time to find materials, and time to monitor progress. The best instruction is to develop an individualized plan for every student. However, even with technology, that is not currently feasible. That is why Westside has developed the flexible action grouping. It allows the staff to use data to group students into small homogenous groups to learn specific skills. Technology not only provides the data for the grouping; it provides some additional time for planning.

> Time is our most valuable resource.

Additional planning time for the teacher is provided when the students go to the computer lab. Westside has a computer technician who runs one of the labs. When students go to the lab, the classroom teacher has that time to work in the classroom. Students are not just sent to the lab to work on the computer. Lab time is when the student receives more individualized attention through technology.

We already know what skills a student has and does not have through assessment data. Using a variety of instructional programs like the Lexia Reading, Compass/Odyssey, keyboarding, and word processing, students work on those skills that they need to practice. If the student does not need practice in the basic skills required for mastery of our standards, the student is put into enrichment programs.

# Computer Labs

Westside has 228 students in grades kindergarten through fifth grade and 110 student work stations. All the workstations have internet access and access to all the programs in the labs. There are two, twenty-five-station PC labs, a ten-station PC lab in the title I room, and an additional ten-station PC lab in the resource room. Each classroom also has three student PC's. The two main

> Computer labs are more manageable than classroom computers.

labs allow all the students in a classroom or grade level to utilize a computer at the same time. They also allow students access to a computer on a daily basis. It took a lot of effort over several years to equip Westside with the two labs. The two labs make it possible for the teachers to do more collaboration, to keep the grade-level teachers aligned on curriculum, to get all the students using technology, and to provide assessment data quickly.

I have asked kindergarten through third grade to spend ninety minutes a week on the computer, preferably in three, thirty-minute blocks. Fourth and fifth grades spend a minimum of thirty minutes a day on the computer. We have found that when computer time is focused on remediation and enrichment of skills, prescribed by the teacher, student learning is greatly increased. We also use this time to teach our keyboarding to second through fourth grade. The fifth-grade students do all their writing using Microsoft Word. This often puts them into one of the labs for an additional time period each day.

The time the students spend in the computer lab is now "free" time for the teachers. The teachers use this time to plan lessons, develop materials for the lessons, review data, and to monitor how the students are progressing in the lab.

I can honestly say that the students enjoy lab time. This is the computer generation. Programs like Lexia, All The Right Type, Power Point, and Word are fun. They keep the students engaged and working hard because the students know the programs are helping them learn or to be better at doing what is being required of them. Our student writing has improved dramatically since they have been allowed to use the computer as a word processor.

The third grade and, to some extent, second grade are now starting to ask for more lab time, mainly for keyboarding and word processing. Those students are asking to do their writing on computers. Since Westside does not have enough room for another lab, we researched portable lap-top labs and other types of technology for word processing. Westside decided to add a lab of AlphaSmart word processors. They are much less expensive, and they hold up very well to the day-to-day use in a classroom environment. There is an added advantage to the AlphaSmart in that, when they download their documents to their folders on the network, it increases their working knowledge of technology.

When the student completes an assignment on the AlphaSmart (all the special education students already use one), they use an infrared beam to transfer the document to a computer in the classroom. The student then puts the document into his or her folder on the network. Once the document is in the folder, the student can edit and print it from any computer in the building.

In addition to the computer labs, each classroom has had three networked student machines for several years. The problem for the teacher was always what to do with the rest of the class while three students were using the classroom computers. It really is a management problem. With our flexible grouping, it is not necessary to use these machines as a station or center. The classroom machines had been used primarily for taking Accelerated Reading comprehension tests. This is starting to change as the teachers become more accustomed to using classroom data. The classroom machines are starting to be used by students for more than taking Accelerated Reading tests. The Lexia and Compass/Odyssey programs are allowing teachers to use the classroom machines to give more remediation and enrichment to individual students during whole group instruction time. Even with flexible grouping, some students still finish a task much sooner than others. They now go to the classroom computer to work on lessons prescribed by the teacher.

## Technology Is a Tool

Technology is a tool, just like textbooks. As teachers become better at individualizing instruction, technology will be used more and more. This is the communication age; students are motivated and in-tune with technology. It is quickly moving from an extra to an integral piece of the school day.

The paradigm shift comes when the staff changes from assuming that all learning takes place in the classroom directed by the teacher to using technology to extend or remediate what the teacher has already taught. When the teacher uses data to prescribe what the student is doing on the computer and frequently monitors what is happening on the computer, individualization is taking place.

Technology is a great tool to help a teacher individualize by providing data for placement and providing practice, remediation, and enrichment. Technology also provides planning time for the teacher.

# 8

# PROVIDING ENRICHMENT

Providing enrichment has had an even greater impact on school climate and student responsibility than we had anticipated. Westside chose not to have a gifted and talented program; we chose instead to design an enrichment program. A gifted and talented program is designed to exclude students who do not meet specific criteria. By having an enrichment program, we were able to define the criteria to include more students.

For several years, the staff and I had often discussed how the low achievers received all the extra help and resources while those students that consistently did well were often asked to work on their own or to do more of the same. We had tried several programs where the classroom teacher was supposed to challenge this group. The teachers worked hard to accomplish this; but in a typical classroom, there simply is not enough time to address the needs of the high group. There is always too much pressure to get the low achievers to pass the class.

## Enrichment Versus Gifted and Talented

When the Wyoming legislature mandated that all students had to pass standards, each school was required to submit an at-risk plan to the Wyoming Department of Education. Wyoming even provided additional funding, the equivalent of one teacher, for at-risk students.

Our frustration at not being able to meet the needs of the high group led us to add a special category to our at-risk plan. Any student who continually passed the standards the first time was considered at-risk. The basis for this was research showing that high-achieving students often become bored with school, creating a potential drop-out in later grades. This definition allowed us to hire, with the new money, a half-time enrichment/at-risk teacher. This teacher works from 11 a.m.

to 4 p.m., Monday through Thursday. The student's day is from 8:15 to 3:00. The enrichment teacher works from 11:00 to 3:00 with students meeting our at-risk criteria for dropping out. From 3:00 to 4:00, she/he is in charge of our after-school tutor program as outlined in Chapter 3, *Developing an At-Risk Program*.

As a staff, we decided the classroom teachers would select who would attend the enrichment class based on our at-risk criteria. Each grade level would have a daily, thirty-minute enrichment block. Students sent to the enrichment room would be responsible for classroom work as well as work from the enrichment room. The enrichment teacher was directed to focus instruction on the application of skills already passed in the classroom using a cross-curricular project approach. Each grade level could send up to twelve students. We would have sent more students, but the room we had available would only hold twelve students. In reality, there are usually eight to twelve students being sent for enrichment.

> Enrichment is to include students, gifted and talented is to exclude students.

The groups are not static. At the completion of a "project," the classroom teacher can change who is going. Since our reading program was already very individualized, math has become the main area for enrichment. The projects are cross-curricular involving math, reading, writing, social studies, and science. In the first, second, and third grades, the enrichment teacher has become part of the flexible action grouping team. Our reading program (basically Accelerated Reading) is already a self-paced reading program that the whole school uses. The need for enrichment in reading is handled very well by the classroom teacher using the Accelerated Reading program.

## Enrichment Teacher Gains Skills

In the past five years, I have had four different teachers in this position. It has become a training ground for staff moving into a regular classroom. The first three enrichment teachers have all moved into regular classrooms. They have all wanted to stay with the enrichment program, but since it is a half-time position, the full-time position is too attractive.

Every time I hire a new person for this position, I give them the same advice. "You are getting the sharpest kids in school. You really have to challenge them. Your current expectations are not high enough for this group, so spend the first few weeks really seeing what they can do." I also ask the new teacher to spend a lot of time communicating with the classroom teacher since these students are required to complete everything in the regular classroom. The enrichment teacher needs to monitor what is happening in the classroom and help the students learn how to stay caught-up. They also need to involve the classroom teachers when planning the projects to ensure the enrichment projects are asking the students to apply skills that have already been taught.

The last area we discuss is grading. We do not give an enrichment grade for the report card since these students already have an "A" in the classroom. I encourage the enrichment teacher to use rubrics so the students know what is expected from them. Projects can be graded based on the rubric, but the classroom teacher does not receive a grade from the enrichment teacher. The focus is on learning and doing, not earning a grade.

> **Enrichment is not graded for the report card.**

Every new teacher has listened attentively and left without a lot of questions. After seven to eight weeks, each has come back to me with essentially the same statement, "Now, I understand what you were saying. These kids get it the first time I teach it. Many of them already knew the answer before I taught it. It took me awhile to get them past earning a grade for the time spent with me, but once that happened, it really started being fun."

Since the students are not "graded," they are more willing to take chances. For many of them, this is the first time they have really tried to achieve. They like the challenge, and they like the feeling of actually learning how to apply skills they already know.

One of the exciting developments with the program is the idea of pre-teaching. A good example was a third grade unit on measurement. One of the measurement standards is using perimeter, area and circumference. The third-grade enrichment group really delved into the standard. They found the area and volume of all types of shapes, including circles. This was done before the regular classroom teacher did whole group instruction on the measurement standard. When the classroom teachers started the measurement unit, they had twelve experts to help them. Using the student experts and hands-on activities, all the students learned how to figure area and volume. The classroom teacher only "tested" up to the standard. All the students learned much more than required to pass the standard, and all the students passed the assessment the first time it was given.

Using peers to help teach is a well-documented technique. Teaching beyond the standard being measured does not take much more time, and it helps students better understand the standard. This idea is discussed more fully in Chapter 6, *Focusing on Standards and Benchmarks*. Not only are more students learning more, the students themselves are becoming part of our learning community.

# Flexible Grouping and Enrichment

The second part of our enrichment program is in response to the "problem" that developed the second year of our flexible action grouping. In the second year, we found that at least half of the students did not need any remediation. What would we do with those students during the flexible action grouping time? We decided to provide enrichment. During flexible action group time, some groups worked on math enrichment by the application of math skills, much like we were already doing in the enrichment program. Reading presented a different problem.

Our Accelerated Reading program already had most of our students reading independently two to four grade levels above their grade and passing the comprehension tests on what they were reading. It didn't seem that more reading would be a good use of their time. We decided that writing was a higher-level application of reading. Westside has three teachers trained as 6-Traits of Writing trainers. 6-Traits of Writing is a writing program developed by Ruth Culham from the Northwest Regional Laboratory in Portland, Oregon. The program focuses on six areas of writing: ideas, organization, voice, word choice, sentence fluency, and conventions. Using the expertise of our trainers, we moved the students that did not need remediation in reading into writing. This became the model for reading enrichment, especially at the fourth-grade and fifth-grade levels.

The number of students receiving enrichment during the flexible action grouping changes each year. This has been another adjustment for the staff. What is being taught and who is being taught really changes when you start using data to guide instruction. The longer a teacher uses data, the easier it is for them to adjust to the student's identified needs; however, the process never becomes "easy" or automatic. When one moves into flexible action grouping to provide for identified needs or to provide enrichment, a lot of planning is required. The school structure has to be changed to provide teachers with the time they need for planning.

# 9

# CREATING A POSITIVE CLIMATE

In the eighties and nineties, Westside worked hard at creating a positive climate for the students. We were successful at making the students feel good about school. Even though many students did not do well academically, they still had great self-images. In other words, even though many kids were doing poorly, scoring in the bottom two quartiles on our norm-referenced testing, they felt good about themselves.

Today, when staff members from other schools visit Westside, they always comment on how well behaved our students are and how much, even the fifth graders, seem to enjoy learning. These comments are not unexpected because now the kids know that they are working hard and that they are truly being successful. Their self-esteem is now based on actual accomplishment.

## Kids Want to Learn

The kindergarten student comes to school excited about learning. In the past, schools have tended to knock that excitement for learning out of them, a little bit each year.

In a typical class of high, middle-high, middle-low, and low achievers, the high achievers and middle-high lost the excitement because they got bored and were seldom challenged. They often did not receive the attention and help that the other groups did. The low group was constantly being asked to do work they were not prepared to do and, in many cases, did not even understand. In order to give them extra help, we identified them to the rest of the students by sending them to a different room, Title I, for part of the day. We even put them into special reading groups in the regular classroom. In our effort to help, our actions reinforced the idea that the low students were not very smart and could not do the work in the regular classroom.

The high group was basically bored to death. They were being successful but were often ignored. Being successful meant you got to do more of the same or had more time to read independently. The teacher's success was measured against the middle-low group, so instruction was aimed at the middle-low group, which did not challenge the students in the high and middle-high groups. Success for the high and middle-high came too easy to be really meaningful to many of those students.

The traditional school structure makes it very difficult for a classroom teacher to provide instruction, feedback, and meaningful work to all four groups at the same time. The high group and middle-high group often did "more of the same," while the low-middle and low group received challenging work, remediation, and attention.

None of the groups really felt that the school was their school. School was a place they spent seven hours a day under the thumb of their teacher, and the teacher controlled every minute of the day, except recess. For many students, even recess was often difficult due to the social learning taking place. The teacher was responsible for the students learning, behavior, and motivation; therefore, very few students took the responsibility for those actions.

> Students are responsible for using their time wisely.

## Climate Changed as Structure Changed

The Westside climate changed for a number of reasons. The changes revolved around giving students more freedom, more challenging work, more involvement in the school, and especially, providing them with the tools to be more successful. The students are successful at Westside due to our at-risk program, flexible action grouping, teaching to standards, and the use of technology.

Now, our daily structure gives the students a lot of individual freedom. As they go to the different purposeful activities during the day, they are moving, not only their bodies, but also their minds. This movement gives students a sense of freedom and control. The expectation is that they will be responsible for using time wisely and effectively. Teaching to standards provides the goals that students work toward. These goals provide one reason for the students to be at school, and they also give students a real sense of accomplishment as they are met.

## A Community Needs Traditions

School should be a community—a community in which everyone, students, staff, and parents, feel they belong, are important, and can contribute to the wellness of the group. Every community has traditions that reflect what is important to that community, and they guide expectations for the community. One of our oldest traditions, aimed at building a positive climate, is the student council.

Westside has had a student council for over twelve years. It has six officers elected from the fourth and fifth grades by the whole student body and a room representative from each of the first-grade through fifth-grade classrooms. The officers are elected at the end of the year for the following year. After a week of campaigning, the candidates have to give a speech in front of all the students explaining their platform. At the end of the day, ballots, with pictures to help the kindergartners, are given to all students; and the voting takes place. Room representatives are elected at the start of the next year.

Being on student council has become a big deal, an important tradition, to the students and to the parents. One year, the Governor of Wyoming helped with the voting. We have also had the Wyoming Superintendent of Schools, college presidents, school board presidents, and mayors visit Westside to teach the student council how to run a meeting using parliamentary procedure and how to get things done using committees. We have even had the local college student body officers run a workshop for our student council.

## Student Council

I have tried to make being on student council important. I send out personal letters to the parents of council members throughout the year on what a great job is being done, what great leadership is being shown, and what is being learned. I also publish in my weekly newsletter what is happening in student council, usually with pictures.

The officers are president (fifth), vice president (fourth), secretary (fifth), Treasurer (fourth), and two historians (fifth and fourth). Each classroom has a room representative. The room representatives are responsible for providing communication to and from their class-room by reading the council minutes to their class, bringing ideas and concerns from the class to student council, and serving on committees.

> Student Council gives students a voice in the school.

The student council meets every two weeks during lunch. The sponsor helps guide them as they conduct their business based on the constitution that was written years ago but is reviewed the first of every year. The student council runs a school store and usually has one large fundraiser every year. The money is used to support activities that involve the whole school. I really try to use the student council in real ways. If at all possible, I forward requests from teachers, parents, and community members to the student council. They often decide on special assemblies, conduct surveys, and determine school participation in special events and activities like fundraisers.

Being on student council means that the student will miss a lot of recesses. He/she will also miss classroom work, which has to be made-up. It is a leadership position, so the expectations are high for behavior and academic grades. However, the rewards are many: more freedoms, more responsibility, more say in how the school is run, and their name on a plaque with all the past student council members.

## School Newspaper

A few years ago, I added a school newspaper. The newspaper is an after-school activity for fifth graders. It was conceived as a way to challenge those students who were really good writers. It has gone from an issue every three months to a monthly. It covers Westside from a student's perspective. My at-risk/enrichment teacher is the sponsor.

There are six editors for the school paper, and fourth-grade students apply for the positions. Students interested in becoming an editor must submit an application to the current staff and go through an interview. The current staff then selects the editors for the next year. We have always had more applicants than positions.

While the actual work is done after school, the training at the start of the year is done during school time. The editors are trained in using one of our digital cameras and several computer programs used to produce the newspaper. When the main editor assigns a story, the story editor often misses class time to cover the event, like a special field trip in another class. The person covering the story is responsible for the classroom work missed and, of course, maintaining good grades and great behavior. The editors work hard and put in a lot of time outside of school to produce their newspaper. Their reward is seeing their writing in print, getting more freedom, and having their picture added to the newspaper wall of fame. The paper is given to all the students and to each administrator and board member in our district.

While the newspaper staff is limited to only six, fifth-grade students, they usually are our top students. Being on the newspaper staff is a big deal to the rest of the students. These six are leaders, and they model high expectations for the rest of the students just like our student council members.

## Bucket-Pals

Another tradition we have at Westside is our buddy or bucket-pal program. It was started years ago to foster a sense of community in order to help cut back on discipline problems between primary and intermediate grades at recess. It continues today even though those grades are now separated at recess.

About once a month, students across grade levels get together for projects, assemblies and activities. Each fifth grader has been paired with a second grader, fourth with a first, and third with a kindergartner. The older students are told that they are role models for the younger students. All the students like the activities. Older students really enjoy helping the younger students, and the younger students really do look up to the older ones. Even though they do not share recess any longer, they still see one another in school and out of school. I always see the older student stand a little straighter when his younger buddy is around.

> Students are encouraged to be role models.

## Peer Reading

Another community builder has been our reading program. At the start of the year, the kindergarten and first-grade students need help taking Accelerated Reading tests. We ask for fourth-grade and fifth-grade volunteers to spend a few minutes in the morning helping those students with their reading. The fourth-grade student will often take a first-grade book home and practice reading it. The next day, he reads it orally to the first grader. They then read the book together, and then the first grader reads the book to the older student. The older student then helps the first grader take the Accelerated Reading test over the book. We have lots of volunteers for this program, so the older kids do not have to worry about falling behind. Most of the time spent on this is while the rest of the students are on the morning walk.

# Presidential Award

Traditions are a big part of school climate. Over the years, I have been able to establish a couple of other traditions aimed at raising expectations. One such tradition is the Presidential Academic Achievement award. When we first started using it, I made it a big deal at our end-of-the-year awards assembly. Each year, a plaque with all the names of the recipients is placed in the main hall. In 1989, we started with about 25% of the students receiving the award; we are now consistently over 50%. At the start of each year, I set the expectation for this award with the fourth-grade and fifth-grade students and their parents by explaining the award and picturing it in my weekly newsletter.

# 150-Point Club

Another tradition that grows each year is the 150-point plaque for our reading wall. Every year, all the students who earn 150 Accelerated Reading points or more get their name, grade, and number of points on a plaque. Each year, I have more students hitting the 150-point mark. In 1989, there were eight names on the plaque. In 2005, fifty-two names were on the plaque. A typical first-grade or second-grade library book is worth one-half point. Many of Westside's first-grade students reach 150 points. That means they have read at least 300 books during the school year.

Students are aware of the plaque and work hard (read a lot of books) to get their name on the plaque. I even have a number of students shooting to get on the plaque every year, including kindergarten and first grade. I know I said students, but what has happened is many parents have bought into this tradition. The parents push their kids to meet the 150 points. Since Accelerated Reading is such an individualized program, every student is working at his/her own reading level. I can honestly say that I have not noticed that our reading expectations are too high. The usual comment I receive from parents is, "Thank you for helping my son/daughter become such a great reader."

# Reading Banner

A more recent tradition, in its fourth year now, is our reading banner. The student who earns the most Accelerated Reading points in the school has their picture, name, grade, year, and number of points put on a large banner which hangs in the library. Each year, there have been several students in competition for this honor. Not only does it keep those high students motivated to keep working, but the banner also becomes a reminder to all students that reading is important and valued by the school community.

## Discipline as a Tradition

Two other programs that have really helped make a positive climate are our discipline program and our bully program. Our discipline program has been used for several years now. It is called "Time to Teach" out of Great Falls, Montana. "Time to Teach" is based on two premises: first, students are not allowed to take valuable teaching time away by being disruptive; and second, students do not come to school knowing how to behave, so we have to teach them. The first couple of weeks of school, all students are taught what the teacher expects of them (these expectations are consistent throughout the building). The students are taught how to get a drink, how to raise their hand, how to go through the lunch line, how to sharpen their pencil, how to walk down the hall, how to play on the recess equipment, and so forth.

> Consistency is the key to effective school discipline.

As a staff, we have tried to identify all those little things we expect from students during the school day, agreed on what we expect, and then taught the students our expectations. One of my duties each year is to show the new kindergarten boys how to use the bathroom facilities. We all go into the bathroom where we talk about germs, how to "aim," how to wash hands, how to be polite, how to throw the paper towel away, and all of those little details that usually go wrong if they are not taught to the students.

If the student does not meet expectations, after one warning, he is sent to a refocus in another classroom. He does not interrupt the instruction in the refocus classroom. He takes a desk and answers four questions on a piece of paper: what did I do wrong, what did it cause to happen, what will I do next time, and am I ready to go back to class. When the refocus teacher has time, she will check the answers and then send him back to class.

When we first adopted the program, the staff, parents, and I identified our absolutes for Westside. An absolute was a discipline problem that results in either in-school or out-of-school suspension. We initially identified seven absolutes: weapons, drugs, physical abuse, verbal abuse, threatening, and disrespect. After the incident at Columbine, Colorado, I added bullying.

Our discipline program is now a tradition. The students know what is expected of them, and parents know what we expect. I must say that I have become spoiled.

I very seldom have a discipline problem in my office. Most of my discipline involves talking to students to prevent a future problem.

## A Bully Program Is Essential

Westside's bully program was developed by our district psychologist and me in response to all the research that came out after the Columbine shooting. We collected all the packaged programs, research, and articles on bullying that we could find. I made a few suggestions, and the psychologist developed the program. It is a first-grade through fifth-grade program that ties into our discipline program. Each year, the psychologist teaches the students, in a few lessons, how to recognize bullying, why a student is a bully, how to react to a bully, and the most important part, how to get help if you are bullied.

All the teachers and support staff in the building receive the same training. The first couple of years of the program, we also held parent meetings to go over the program with them. Now, I cover the program in my newsletters. The amount of bullying taking place at Westside has declined dramatically over the years as students and parents have become more in-tune with our expectations. Now, I very seldom have a boy that I have to work with due to bullying. My biggest problem has become girls and their social bullying. The psychologist is continually making special lessons for hot spots that develop. Special lessons on the way girls bully have been given at each grade level. We have even had several group counseling sessions with specific girls to provide help to those girls being bullied. The point here is that one program does not work for all students. You have to continually monitor and adjust to meet the ever-changing needs of the students.

The bully program started as a reaction to a tragic event, Columbine. Through our bully program, I have become very aware of how schools need to be safe. Bullying is not a "rite of passage." It is destructive to so many students for a very long time. This really became clear to me when I did a program at our Rotary Club about our bully program.

At the end of the program, many of the Rotarians were very concerned that the bully program was hurting the kids, not letting them experience lessons that would help them later in life. The other half of the club was very supportive of the program and wanted to know if it was in the other elementary schools. On the way back to Westside, I realized which group was the "bullies" when they were in school and which group got "bullied."

# 10

# USING PARENT COMMUNICATION TO DEVELOP SUPPORT

I moved to Powell, in 1984, to become the first, full-time principal at Westside. As I was looking for a home, several realtors would only show me homes outside of the Westside attendance area. I was told that Westside was the school where all the teachers that were "trouble-makers" were sent. Obviously, they were quite embarrassed when they learned why I had come to Powell. Needless to say, as the new Westside principal, one of my first goals was to change the perceived image of the school.

## Changing the Perception

After meeting my new staff and getting to know them, I realized that the perception of the staff by the community was not accurate. The staff was composed of individuals who all cared for the students and wanted to do the best job they could. They had been labeled unfairly because they often questioned the status-quo. It quickly became apparent to me that Westside had several of the best teachers in the district, and I wanted the community to know how fortunate their children were to attend Westside.

Five years later, the realtors were promoting Westside, as were our parents. This change in community perception did not come about because we changed how or what was being taught. It came about because we started including parents in what we were doing and letting people know about the things occurring at

Westside. We encouraged parents to become involved with the school; we really started to communicate with them.

To help change the community perception of Westside, I tried to have our special activities covered in our local paper. When a teacher was doing a unique lesson or **Perception too easily becomes reality.** activity with her class, I would call the reporter and invite him to come and watch. This usually led to a picture and short article in the paper. It was good for their circulation and for Westside.

At first, I just made sure Westside activities were featured in the local paper. Later, I added my own newsletter, sent home with the students, highlighting special activities and events. Slowly, the public's perception began to change.

## Parent Involvement is Critical

Parents are generally hesitant to come to school. As the principal, I believe it is my responsibility to develop ways for parents to be drawn to the school and to ensure that they are comfortable when they are at school. Fortunately, Westside already had an active, supportive parents group that had been organized to support students. Over the years, the group has consisted of from two or three active parents up to a dozen. They have all worked hard to add value to the school through activities and support for the students.

The parents group usually has two fundraising activities a year. In the fall, they run a book fair during our first parent-teacher conferences; and in the spring, they have a spaghetti dinner. The spaghetti dinner is combined with a dessert auction that has always been a terrific fundraiser. The fifth-grade students get involved with the dinner as the waiters and waitresses. The parents really enjoy watching the kids "work," and the kids really enjoy the responsibility.

The parents group uses the funds to support school activities. They provide scholarships for all the school activities requiring student fees. They have helped purchase special software, like our Compass program, and hardware, like digital cameras for each grade level.

This group also provides the staff with a carry-in dinner during the week of conferences, since these meetings are in the evening. They also make sure the staff is recognized during National Education week and National Teacher Appreciation week. This kind of support for the students and the staff has made a positive impact on student achievement. The students and staff know the parents are supportive of what is happening at Westside.

I view my role as a support person, information person and at times, a guide. I have always appreciated the parents who are willing to give so much time and energy to helping all the students.

## Back-to-School Night

Almost every school has a back-to-school night or open house to introduce the school staff to parents. The first two years, I just followed the previous tradition. All the staff and parents would gather in the gym one evening in early fall. I would introduce the staff to the parents and give a short welcome. Then, the staff and parents went to the classroom for more rules and regulations. It was a public relations disaster. We came off as cold and distant. My third year, we started to change the structure of the evening so that it was a more positive experience for everyone involved.

Back-to-school night became a night for the students to show off their school to their parents, no more big meetings in the gym. I welcomed parents as they entered the school, and the kids showed them around. It was their school, and the kids loved showing their parents every part of it. When they went to the classroom to meet the teacher, they received a sheet with the rules and regulations on it. The teachers talked about what exciting things were going to happen during the year. Later, this developed into a class syllabus that contained all the special events, activities, dates, field trips, and grading criteria for that grade.

In addition to the class syllabus, we now have a building handbook. The handbook is more of a how-to book than a rules book. Not only does it contain the how's and why's of running a school, but it also has our yearly calendar and all the students' birthdays (by parent permission) listed on the calendar. The handbook is given out during our open house. Occasionally, I do meet with all the parents and kids in the gym for important messages, to explain new standards and policies, or to go over a new program. I make these presentations short and tied to a lively power-point. Then, everyone goes to the classrooms.

As a side note, during my fourth year, with around 320 students, the parents group helped me organize a carry-in dinner for our open house. It was terrific. Looking back, this is when everyone, students, parents, and staff, started to look at Westside as a community. It was also the time when our average scores on the old SRA norm-referenced test jumped from the 30th to 40th percentile to the 50th to 60th percentile. This happened even though we really had not made any curriculum changes. I mention this because school climate and parent involvement really do make a difference in learning. Over the years, things have continued to change, and the carry-in went away as we got more and more single parents and low income families.

## End-of-Year Barbeque

As we did away with the carry-in, we added an end-of-the-year barbecue for staff, students, and volunteers. The barbecue came about as a way to have fun on the last day of school and to thank all the volunteers for their help throughout the year. Our first barbecue was a real team effort. We had twelve home grills working to serve over 400 hamburgers, with staff members and parents doing the cooking. The kids and parents loved it. I still remember everyone sitting around on the grass eating lunch—parents, students, and staff. It was just like the family reunion barbecues I remembered from my youth. I can't remember a discipline problem during any of the barbecues. The barbecue is also a way to send the kids home for the summer with a positive memory of school. That emotion will help them want to come back in the fall. After a few years, our barbecue became a tradition in all five of the Powell schools.

Our last day has now become a fun day for students. In the morning, we have our awards assembly which begins with a slide show containing 140–150 pictures of students taken throughout the year. During the school year, the teachers and I take pictures of all the activities and learning going on at Westside. These photos are saved on a server accessible to all staff. I put together a twelve minute power-point with captions and music that tries to capture the past year. The kids love it. They end school by remembering all the fun things they have done. Next, we go to our barbecue lunch and then end with the afternoon activities, which the parents plan and supervise. The teachers go from station to station with their students, while the parents do all the "work." It is a great time for everyone. The entire day is aimed at creating a very positive memory for the students. That memory makes them miss school and want to return in the fall.

## Movie Night

In just the last few years, the parents group started a movie night. The movies are shown every few weeks in the gym and are free to all. The parents group sells concessions. Westside had a DVD player and a projector, so the first year we borrowed a sound system from the high school. The second year, the student council purchased a high-end portable sound system which is also used for assemblies. Now, the student council surveys the students a couple of times a year to decide which movies to show. The only rule for movie night is that someone twelve or older has to accompany the student. The kids bring pillows and blankets, so that they can lie on the floor to watch the movie. The movie is always on a Friday night. Many groups come that are on a sleepover or birthday party. The seating behind the kids on the floor is filled with the adults, and we usually have eighty to one-hundred people at movie night.

I truly enjoy movie night. All I have to do is "run" the movie. There has yet to be a discipline problem. It is our community enjoying being at their school for a positive experience. What is really fun is having a former Westside graduate, now in middle school or high school, come to watch the movie as the adult with a younger sibling.

## New-Parent Night

In 2002, the staff and I realized that Westside had high expectations for students and parents. Parents new to Westside were having a hard time learning all the expectations in a timely manner. To alleviate this problem, new-parent night was developed. A couple of weeks after our back-to-school night, the parents organization hosts a new-parent night. I send personal invitations to all the parents who are new to Westside. The sixty-minute meeting is for parents. To encourage more parents to attend, the parents group provides babysitting in the gym.

> It is important to educate new parents so they feel part of the school.

The kindergarten teacher and I explain the Westside philosophy, why education is so important, and how our main programs work, including the discipline program, Accelerated Reading, student council, enrichment and standards. At the end, we answer questions and then have refreshments. There is always a sixty percent to seventy-five percent turn-out. I have had parents come up to me two years later and express how much they enjoyed and appreciated new-parent night.

## Parents Lunch at School

Parents are encouraged to occasionally eat lunch with their child. During the year, about 60 percent of the parents take advantage of this opportunity. Parents have to purchase their own lunch and sit with the students. The kids love to have their parents eat lunch with them. I enjoy watching the parent, surrounded by kids vying for their attention, trying to eat with all the conversations being directed at them.

## Welcome Letter

The teachers have all developed their own ways to show parents how much they value the students and parent participation in school. Every teacher now sends a letter or postcard to their new students every summer. It is just a note telling the student how much fun it will be next fall having them in their class.

Over the years, postcards have been sent from places like Ireland, Italy, Hawaii, Alaska, and Australia. These postcards have really helped the students develop a desire to return to school. I willingly pay for the postage. In fact, on the teachers' last day, I hand out stamps and the addresses of their next year's students.

## Newsletters

My occasional newsletter has developed into a one-page, weekly newsletter with pictures. I try to have no more than three short articles about the great things happening at Westside. I tie in our use of grant money, changes in the school and student achievement. I also keep parents informed about state and district mandates, how we are funded, what parents are volunteering to do, and what the students are doing at school, with accompanying photos. The newsletter is also sent to all the administrators and board members in the district, our local paper, our local state representatives and senators, and the state superintendent of schools.

A few years ago, I asked each teacher to do a monthly newsletter. I felt it was important for the teacher to let the parents know what their child would be doing at school the following month. One year, the parents group purchased a digital camera for each grade level. They felt the teachers' newsletters would be improved if they contained pictures of the kids. I purchased a color printer for one of our labs so the teachers could develop their pictures. That fall, I started school with a half-day in-service on how to use the camera, download digital photos and insert photos into a document.

The teacher newsletters are improving each year. Since many teachers are now sending out several a month, always with pictures of special lessons or activities that are taking place in the classroom, each grade level needed its own color printer. There have been several benefits from having the cameras. There is a lot more collaboration between grade-level teachers, and they work together to produce a newsletter for the grade. The teachers are getting more proficient using technology. In fact, many

> Teachers use newsletters with pictures to communicate with parents.

are starting to teach the students how to use the camera, so they have a room photographer to document what's happening.

In addition, several teachers are now making student portfolios. Using pictures from the digital camera and the color printer, they document what the student did during the school year. The music and P.E. teachers also have cameras and produce a newsletter.

These experiences have made me realize how important it is to keep parents informed and involved with what is happening at school. When you get the students involved, the results are even more impressive. Helping with the newsletters is just another way for students to feel they are responsible for what happens in school. Instead of the teacher giving them information, they are starting to feel they are part of a team aimed at helping them learn. This translates into higher expectations and higher student achievement.

## Letters from the Principal

If our parents receive a letter from the principal, it's likely to be positive. I enjoy recognizing students when they reach a milestone in their reading, attain a student council office, show leadership, master a standard that has been particularly difficult, or get their picture in the local paper. These opportunities allow me to show the parents, and students, that we notice when their child excels.

## Parents Know What Is Expected

These are a few of the ways that we communicate with parents. This communication helps parents understand what we are doing at Westside. When parents know what is going on, they tend to trust us and want to help us. Our high expectations for learning would not mean a thing if the parents did not support what we are trying to achieve.

The staff at Westside works hard to communicate how the students are doing academically. As a standards-driven school, all the parents receive a copy of the grade-level standards and benchmarks at our fall open house. The expectation that all students will pass all the standards and benchmarks is clearly communicated. As soon as a student runs into difficulty passing a standard or benchmark, the parent is notified. Most often, that notification is accompanied with a request to put the student into our at-risk program. Notification is handled through a phone call or a face-to-face conference. The problem is discussed along with what the teacher will do to help and what the parent can do to help. It is the exception that the parent will not help us.

I have always believed that parents need to be involved with school. Schools have a choice: they can either get parents involved in a positive way, by making them a part of the educational process, or deal with them in an adverse way because they do not understand what is happening at school or why things are being done at school. Both take the same amount of time. After 30 years of trying different approaches, I know parents have to be involved if all students are going to achieve at a high level. Strong parental involvement is another attribute of a category three school. It really does take a community to educate a child: parents, students, and teachers.

# 11

# CHANGING EXPECTATIONS

I believe that expectations are the hardest area to change when one starts down the road to real school improvement, moving from a category two academic school (students achieving in the 50th to 70th percentile) to a category three academic school (students achieving in the 70th to 90th percentile). Just how hard it is to change expectations really became apparent to me as the Westside third grade started to use flexible grouping.

## Expectations versus Experience

Third grade was already using data from Compass/Odyssey to group students for remedial instruction aimed at achieving mastery of our reading benchmarks. They were also using the Accelerated Reading program, and the students had shown excellent gains over the past two years. When they put their students into flexible action groups, it pro- duced even greater stu- dent achievement in read- ing. Comparing Terra Nova test results from the end of second grade to the end of third grade showed more than a year's growth for every student. Comparing the previous third-grade results to this third grade, the one using flexible action grouping showed an average gain of one year six months in the reading composite score. The average reading level was now above the fifth-grade level.

> Flexible grouping increases achievement.

That spring, I went to the fourth-grade teachers to let them know how well their next year's students were doing. I shared the test results with them, the gain over the previous year's students, and what a super year they should have next year. That fall, I again shared all the information with them.

After waiting a few weeks, I went back to the fourth-grade teachers to see what was happening. During our conference, they told me that they really could not see any difference between this class and previous classes, even though test results showed this group had an average of almost a two-year advantage in reading.

Both of these teachers are excellent, and their test scores are consistently the best in the state in reading, math, and writing. I reflected on this and decided that, even though the students had changed, expectations and class structure had not. I did not bring this up to the teachers. The year was well underway, and it was not a good time to try and make major changes.

At the end of the year, I looked at the reading results from this new class of third-graders. The average student achievement again showed the class reading above the fifth-grade level. I went back to the fourth-grade teachers with the new test results. We discussed the test data and what it could mean to instruction. The conversation focused on expecting more from the students because it looked like they were capable of doing more. The next fall, they started with increased expectations, and the students met those expectations.

That fall, I waited a few weeks and then asked them how it was going. After a short hesitation, both exclaimed that this was the best class they could remember. These students could really read. What is especially interesting about this example is that our assessment data indicated that this class was actually not quite as good as the previous year's class.

## Expectations Are Hard to Change

Expectations are extremely difficult to change. Schools are a complex system. Parents, students and teachers are all major parts of that system. For expectations to truly change, they have to change for all groups. The students are great at playing school. They only do as much as you ask. Generally, because of the way schools are run, most students have little intrinsic motivation toward learning; their goal is to do as little as possible to pass the grade. In many cases, parents send their kids to school to be educated, as long as it does not interfere with their lives. That means, many parents do not want unhappy kids who complain about school, and they do not want to help their children with schoolwork at home. Teachers only have so much time during the day. They do the best they can in their school structure. When you put the three groups together, it adds up to low expectations. If you raise the expectations in just one group, the other two will rebel.

## Educate the Parents

The first step at Westside to raising expectations was to build a safety net for those students who would initially fail. Westside's at-risk plan (see Chapter 3) was in place before any other changes were made. The second step was communication with parents. Parents had to know why expectations were going to change and how the school was going to help their child meet those expectations.

> To change expectations, you must first build a safety net.

Getting parents to buy into higher expectations was accomplished by giving them the data on why schooling is so much more important today than even ten years ago in relation to earning a middle-class income. This was accomplished by sharing with parents data related to the changing job market and the skills now needed to earn a middle-class income in a global economy. As I communicated with parents, I found that they basically broke into three groups: those parents who had not even thought about why their child was going to school, the group that "thought" their child would get a job much like theirs, and the third group of parents who already knew why their child was in school and were totally committed to higher expectations. The middle group, those who thought their child would get a job similar to their job, was especially interested since they were already seeing the time when their job would be gone—jobs like working in the oil field, agriculture, and manufacturing. Given the data, this group joined the "going to college" group

> Parents have to be educated along with the students.

and really got behind higher expectations. The first group actually started to think about why their child was in school and what they could do to help them. I have yet to find a parent who does not want their child to be successful. I have found a number of parents who had no idea how to help but were very willing to take suggestions and start helping. The majority of the parents in this group, when given the information on what was needed in today's world to be successful, would do the best they could to support the school's efforts to educate their child. As parents started to see the need for a good education for all students, they communicated that need to their children. Then, we started to raise our expectations.

## Clear Standards Are Important

It is also necessary to have a clear set of standards for each subject and grade level. The parents and students must know the first day of class what is expected of them in order to change expectations. With this expectation, it is easy to develop the idea that school is not a competition and that everyone needs to pass all the standards. Slowly, everyone will buy into the idea that learning is not a competition with winners and losers; it is what is expected for all kids.

This really came home to me one day when I was observing in the Title I room. The teacher was working with four students. They had spent several days working on the remediation of a standard. Today, it was time for the assessment, to see if the students could show mastery of the standard, so they could move to the next standard. Each student was given a copy of the assessment. As they finished, they handed it to the teacher for scoring. The teacher finished correcting the first paper and handed it back to the student with a "Great job, you passed." The other three students spontaneously started clapping. I knew at that moment that Westside had changed from learning as a competition to learning as an expectation for all students. The students had bought into becoming educated. They wanted to learn what was being taught to them.

## At-Risk Program Brings Results

Our at-risk program was accomplishing two important things. The first was to ensure that all students were entering the next grade at or above grade level in reading and math. Second, as the at-risk program became more established and a proven intervention, the teachers started to teach to the middle and upper-middle groups of the class instead of the low or low-middle groups. This was a huge jump in expectations.

Then, something unexpected happened with the students. All the students started to feel they could be successful at grade level. The old adage that success breeds success proved true. Classroom instruction became more exciting. The high group started to actually work harder because they were being taught to and challenged. This required the low groups to work even harder, but they had the foundation in skills and extra support so that as they did work harder they could continue to be successful. This group also had the knowledge that, if they needed it, they could get extra help from our at-risk program. We found that, if we could get the students reading and doing math at

> Teach beyond standards, but only grade the standards.

grade level by the end of third grade, then those students would continue to be at grade level in the fourth and fifth grade. Our focus on basic skills in the primary grades was building a strong foundation for future learning and allowing the upper grades to move into more and more application.

After two years of our at-risk program and flexible action grouping, we actually gained instructional time because we did not have to spend as much class time on remediation or re-teaching. This allowed us to start teaching beyond the standards, especially in math, as explained in chapter 6. It has also encouraged the teachers to raise expectations and the students to take more risks. The students actually try harder because there isn't a risk of failure. The teacher is more relaxed and feels there is time to try new instructional techniques and new materials.

Expectations are difficult to change. To change expectations, one needs to work with all the groups involved and to have a safety net for those who do not achieve the new level of expectation. Without laying the groundwork first, it becomes easy for higher expectations to actually lead to lower achievement. A few students will respond to the increased expectations, while many students, who are already having trouble, just slip lower, creating more students who feel, "I can't do this." This becomes a downward spiral resulting in even lower expectations.

Increasing expectations and sustaining higher expectations is difficult and that is why moving from a category two to a category three school requires a paradigm shift. The parents, students, and staff all have to change how they think and behave.

# 12

# CONCLUSION

No Child Left Behind has brought many changes to education, and from my perspective, many changes that were needed. We have known for many years that all kids can learn; schools just lacked the will to make the changes necessary to accomplish that goal. It has been much easier to continue with the goal of the industrial age, education for some. It has been easier to do what we have always done; change a textbook, invest in the latest instructional technique, or jump into a new program—all the while, maintaining the original structure and schedule.

School improvement is not a goal; it is a process that does not end. As one staff member stated at a staff meeting, "We are nothing if not flexible." She said it with pride. Everyone knew she was saying we really do work together as a team. We use data to determine what the child needs to learn, and we are providing more time and, if needed, a different program to ensure that the child does learn. Our instruction is always changing, based on the changing needs of our students.

The primary goal of No Child Left Behind is to raise achievement, and most schools want to accomplish this by just changing the textbook, adding a new program, or developing a new teaching technique. They want to raise scores without making any real changes in their system or structure. Those types of changes may increase some scores, but they will not take a school beyond a category two level. To reach a category three or four level, you must change the structure of the school, which is a paradigm shift for the staff. This change in thinking requires the staff to use assessment data to place every student on the curriculum continuum and give some students additional time to master the curriculum.

> Curriculum, through standards, is the road all students must travel.

The curricular continuum is the road students take in their journey from kindergarten through twelfth grade. The standards and benchmarks are the mileage posts along the way. When a student misses a mileage post, a standard or benchmark, the probability of completing the journey gets less and less.

## Make Schools a Journey not a Foot Race

Schools have traditionally made the journey a foot race between the students. Everyone started in August, covered the curriculum all year, and ended in May. It didn't matter if a student wasn't ready for the race or if a student was already halfway through the race. They all started at the same place, were given the same amount of time, and ended at the same time. In other words, time was a constant for all students.

In a category three or four school, time has become a variable. Every student still starts at the same time, but the time used to cover the curriculum has become very different. Student progress toward mastery of the curriculum, standards, and benchmarks is closely monitored. Students who need more time are given more time through flexible action groups. This allows the teacher to differentiate instruction for all the students while continuing to move all students along the curriculum continuum. The thirty minutes of daily, direct instruction doesn't increase the separation between students on mastery of the standards. Instead, it allows the ones that need more time to get more time and those that already have mastery to be challenged by applying the benchmarks to higher-level problems.

> A foot race makes winners and losers.

## Collaboration Is a Paradigm Shift

In many ways, the paradigm shift isn't due to how assessment data is used to make a physical change in the use of time during the day; it is due to how the teachers view the students and how they work together. In a traditional school, category one or two, each classroom is an island. There is very little collaboration between teachers in the same grade and almost none between grade levels. In the category three and four schools, the grade-level teachers spend much of their planning time working together to ensure that they are both teaching what needs to be taught, using data to remediate the right benchmarks to the right students, and challenging the rest of the students. It is no longer my classroom or my students; it is our grade and our students.

In a category three or four school, the teacher uses technology as an instructional tool that provides formative data and helps with progress monitoring.

Technology, under the control of the teacher, becomes a very strong instructional tool and actually gives the teacher more time to plan. Using assessment data, the teacher can use technology to help with remediation, enrichment, and practice. Technology extends learning time and presents material in a different learning style, while giving the teacher the additional time to plan and develop lessons aimed at meeting the needs of all the students.

As the school structure changes, so does the school climate. By purposely addressing all the factors that make up the climate, such as, parent relations, discipline, at-risk program, and enrichment, you can create a climate in which the students want to learn. After all, it is human nature to want to learn, to see what is over the next hill. In traditional schools, students are passive learners, causing some students to resist or even fight learning. In a category three or four school, the student is an active part of the teaching and learning process. The climate of the school supports the student's natural desire to learn.

> **Students want to learn; traditional schools often remove that desire.**

## Learning for All Requires a Structural Change

All kids can learn, but it requires a change in the basic school structure. The amount of instructional time for each student has to become a variable. Instructional programs have to be aligned to the student, instead of all students being placed into the same program. Formative data has to be used as a tool by the teacher to design a program for each student.

> **For all students to learn, time must become a variable.**

The teacher and the community need to become passionate about all kids being successful.

Thanks to flexible action grouping and our use of technology, it has become easier to make adjustments to students' programs. Technology helped us identify specific needs, and the flexible grouping and the computer lab made it easier to give those students the specific instruction and additional time they needed to become proficient.

Remember, it takes time to change; sustainable change doesn't happen overnight. Start slowly with changing the school climate and adding an at-risk plan. Bring about the trust you need to change the academic side. In this book, I have tried to outline the basic ingredients that resulted in Westside being chosen as a Blue Ribbon school. To become a school where students, parents, and teachers are all successful, you have to change the structure and the schedule. It is a scary journey, but the rewards are worth it.

# APPENDIX A

## WESTSIDE ELEMENTARY
## STUDENT AT-RISK PLAN
## REVISED 05/03, 01/05

"There is nothing so unequal as the equal treatment of unequals." Joseph Renzulli

Developed by the At-Risk committee: Bonnie Fauskee, Carolyn Danko, Mary Reynolds, Maribeth McCleary, Julie Stingley, Pam Masterson and Brent Walker on March 24, 1998 and revised March, 1999. The Westside Philosophy, adopted in 1991, revised in May 1998, and again in May 2003 is the guide for this at-risk plan.

## Philosophy

In a safe, orderly and positive environment, where learning is valued and differences are accepted, each child will achieve mastery of the district standards and will develop and progress intellectually, socially, emotionally, behaviorally and physically as an individual.

## At-Risk identification

Students "at risk" in Wyoming are defined, according to State Board of Education Rules and Regulations, as individuals of school age who appear likely to fail economically, socially, and academically. At Westside, the staff has also identified students who easily achieve district standards as being "at risk".

# Identification

Identification of students will take place through the district adopted Building Intervention Team referral process. Referrals of At-Risk students to the BIT team may be by teacher, administrator, parent or student. All cases referred will be considered and evaluated on the following criteria:

1.  Students who have been provided documented teaching and reteaching activities and still have not demonstrated mastery of adopted performance standards.

2.  Students whose performance on norm-referenced, standardized tests is below the national average.

3.  Students who consistently meet or exceed expected levels on adopted performance standards on pre or initial assessment.

4.  Students who demonstrate through daily use and assessment that they have Limited English Proficiency.

5.  Students whose environment places them in a position to experience domestic violence.

6.  Students whose behavioral record in the classroom and/or on the playground indicates they are experiencing social dysfunction.

7.  Students who are of Native American heritage.

8.  Migrant Students.

# At-Risk Interventions

Social and Behavioral needs

    a.  DARE—Drugs and Alcohol Resistance Education

    b.  Counseling (group and individual)

    c.  Mentoring (peer and cross-age)

    d.  Discipline plan (building, classroom, and individual procedures which are standardized, emphasize positive interaction with students, and strive to educate regarding acceptable behaviors)

Emotional needs

    a.  Counseling

b.   Therapy groups

c.   Individualized discipline plan

Academic needs

a.   After-school tutoring

b.   Noon catch-up/tutoring

c.   Title I

d.   Special Education

e.   Mentoring

f.   At-Risk Teacher

g.   Accelerated Reading Program

h.   Volunteers

i.   CCC and Compass Learning

j.   Summer School

Enrichment interventions

a.   CCC and Compass Learning Lab

b.   Accelerated Reader

c.   Reading Renaissance

d.   State, Regional, and National Competitions

e.   Enrichment teacher

## Classroom interventions

It is in the classroom where the first interventions take place. When the teacher feels she can no longer meet the additional needs of an at-risk student due to time constraints, number of students in the classroom or the severity of the needs, she will refer the student to the after-school tutor program. If the tutor program does not achieve the desired results the teacher will complete a BIT referral on the student.

Regular classroom planning and instruction will be aimed at ensuring all students will achieve the district adopted performance standards. Students who fail to meet the performance standards or who easily achieve the performance will be identified as being at-risk.

## Classroom use of Highly Qualified Teacher Assistants

There are five, four-hour teacher assistants working in the building. They are assigned to help with specific students and tasks. Some of the duties include help with behaviorally challenged students in the classroom. Some of the other duties are listed below.

- One-to-one conferences with students
- Computer lab supervisor while small groups are word processing, keyboarding, and computerized drill activities.
- Helping Kindergarten through second grade students with Accelerated Reader tests.
- Helping with data collection/management pertaining to standards.
- Helping supervise the students.
- Small group instruction under teacher supervision

## At-Risk Teacher

We are fortunate to be able to employ a ½ time certified teacher to work with At-Risk students. This person is responsible for directing the after-school tutor program and helping all students identified as at-risk. These students present unique needs in that they are the students who don't qualify for special education and have already had extensive remedial work, but will not meet standards without one-to-one or small group instruction. This person also coordinates the building enrichment program. This teacher works from 11:00 to 4:00 Monday through Thursday.

## CCC Lab Manager

The CCC lab manager is in the computer lab to supervise students working in the lab. The lab manager also provides help and instruction in the various computerized programs being utilized for remediation and enrichment. The manager provides teachers with on-going data from the lab for them to use in planning for instruction. The CCC Lab Manager is in the lab at 7:30 a.m. for the before school tutoring program.

# Before School and After School Tutor Program

Westside sets aside over $4,000 each year to help fund the tutoring programs. This money allows Westside to use up to four teacher assistants if they are needed. The programs focus on students completing identified standards. Students are formally referred to this program by the classroom teacher when they complete the after-school tutor referral. The before school program is from 7:30 to 8:15 and the after school program is from 3:00 to 4:00.

# Noon catch-up Program

The noon catch-up program is a 30-minute program which takes place during the noon hour every day. It is staffed by teacher assistants and is in two sections, primary and intermediate. Students are sent (no choice) and allowed (by choice) to go to the noon program. The intent is to give students time to complete work that was supposed to be done at school.

# America Reads Aide

In cooperation with Northwest College, we receive a 2-hour a day aide to help teach reading at the Kindergarten through 3$^{rd}$ grade level. The college pays for the aide through a federally funded program. We use this person to work with individuals and small groups on reading.

# ENRICHMENT OPPORTUNITIES

# Student Newspaper: "The School Scoop"

Fifth grade students can apply for the six staff positions on the school newspaper. The paper staff aims at completing an issue each month.

# Student Council

The student council is the voice of Westside students. Students can and should become involved in **their** school. Each fall every class elects a room representative to serve on student council. Each spring the entire student body elects a president and secretary from fifth grade, and a vice-president and treasurer from fourth grade. Two Historians are elected, one from fourth and one from fifth grade. Through the student council, students are provided with an opportunity to serve in a leadership capacity at all grade levels. The student council, working with the teachers and principal, identify possible ways of improving their school and helping the community.

## Reading Renaissance

The reading renaissance program is tied to the computerized Accelerated Reading program. Students are encouraged to read books at their appropriate reading level. The classroom teacher closely monitors the computerized printouts on how each student is doing with his/her reading. This allows the teacher to help the student choose books appropriate to his/her zone of proximal development, ensuring that the student is making maximum gain in his/her reading development.

## Enrichment Program

Each grade level has a 30 minute slot in the enrichment program. Students are recommended by the teacher for enrichment based on Westside's at-risk criteria. The enrichment teacher provides instruction in math with these students. Most of the instruction is project based aimed at teaching students how to apply the skills they have already mastered in the regular classroom. The projects tend to be cross-curricular.

# REFERENCES

AlphaSmart. Renaissance Learning, Inc. Wisconsin Rapids, WI. (800)656-6740. www.alphasmart.com

CompassLearning, Inc. San Diego, CA. (800)422-4339. www.compasslearning. com

Friedman, Thomas L. *The World Is Flat.* New York, NY: Farrar, Straus and Giroux, 2005

Lexia Learning Systems, Inc. Lincoln, MA. (800)435-3942. www.lexialeaarning. com

Lexotte, W.L. *The Effective Schools Process: A Proven Path to Learning for All.* Okemos, Michigan. Effective Schools Products, Ltd., 1999.

Research Summary. (2002) *Summary of Research Regarding Renaissance School Improvement Process.* Renaissance Learning. Madison, WI. (800)338-4204. www.renlearn.com

STAR Reading, STAR Math, STAR Early Literacy. Renaissance Learning. Madison, WI. (800)338-4204. www.renlearn.com

Time to Teach, Education Development Center. Coeur d' Alene, ID. (208)772-0273

978-0-595-40956-3
0-595-40956-3

Made in the USA